CHILDREN
IN THE
MOVIES

CHILDREN
IN THE
MOVIES
NEIL SINYARD

St. Martin's Press, New York

First published in the United States of America in 1992

Printed in Great Britain

ISBN 0-312-07574-X

Library of Congress Cataloging-in-Publication Data

Sinyard, Neil.
    Children in the movies/Neil Sinyard.
        p.   cm.
    Includes bibliographical references and index.
        ISBN 0-312-07574-X
        1. Children in motion pictures.
        I. Title.
PN1995.9.C4S57   1992
791.43′652054—dc20   91-40558
                                    CIP

ACKNOWLEDGEMENTS

Almost all of the photographs in this book were originally issued to publicize or promote films made or distributed by the following companies, to whom the Author and Publishers gratefully offer acknowledgement: AB Cinematograph, Artificial Eye, Associated British-Pathe, BIP, British Film Institute, British Lion/London Films, Bryanston, Cannon, Columbia, Crown Film Unit, Ealing Studios, EMI/World Film Services, Films du Carrosse, First National, GFD, Mainline Pictures, Metro-Goldwyn-Mayer, Nouvelles Editions, Palace Pictures, Paramount, Pathé, PDS-ENIC, Picnic Productions/ Australia Film Corporation, The Rank Organization, RKO, Road Movies/ Argos, Robert Dorfmann, Samuel Goldwyn, TCF, Thorn EMI, United Artists, Universal-International and Warner Brothers. Gratitude is also extended to the staff of the National Film Archive.

Frontispiece
Tatum O'Neal
in *Paper Moon*

The Railway Children

CONTENTS

INTRODUCTION

> *At all costs the true world of childhood must prevail, must be restored; that world whose momentous, heroic, mysterious quality is fed on airy nothings, whose substance is so ill-fitted to withstand the brutal touch of adult inquisition.*
>
> (JEAN COCTEAU, *Les Enfants Terribles*)

CHILDHOOD is the great universal theme and it is not surprising that some of the greatest films in the history of the cinema, from Bergman to Spielberg, from Tarkovsky to Charles Laughton, have focused on it. Clearly one of its attractions is its appeal to common experience. As Martin Amis once blandly remarked when observing the diversity of age and social background of an audience for *E. T. – The Extra-Terrestrial* (1982), the one thing the audience all had in common was that they had all been children.

For some artists, like Woody Allen in *Radio Days* (1987), childhood provides the route for an aesthetic exploration of nostalgia, and for memories of development or underdevelopment. Others adopt a frankly Romantic approach, in a tradition derived from Blake's *Songs of Innocence* or Wordsworth's *The Prelude*, in which childhood is the site of innocent understanding and instinctive imagination. The Romantic approach in the cinema can manifest itself in different ways, but one of the most powerful and popular has always been to align the child with Nature, whether it be in the form of a close relationship with the animal world – works as diverse as *The Red Pony* (1948), *Kes* (1969) and *The Black Stallion* (1979) are essentially variations on this tradition – or in a straight contrast between the liberating country and the inhibiting city, which is expounded in almost diagrammatic form in John Boorman's *Hope and Glory* (1987).

An alternative to the Romantic approach to childhood is what one might call the Freudian approach. Here the artist proposes that the roots of the adult mind and personality are contained in childhood consciousness and experience, with the child's first vision of the sexual act being a crucial

Jodie Foster as a young moll in Alan Parker's *Bugsy Malone* (1976)

7

formative experience. Because childhood and adulthood in this view are inextricably linked, the artistic structure demands an interweaving, indeed interlocking, of past and present. Joseph Losey's film of L. P. Hartley's *The Go-Between* (1970) is probably the classic example of this, and Dennis Potter's TV screenplay for *The Singing Detective* (1986) is another distinguished case.

These are some of the broad artistic approaches to the theme of childhood, but what does a fascination with childhood reveal about the artist? For one thing, it might simply reveal his reluctance to grow up. In Nicolas Roeg's *Track 29* (1988), scripted by Dennis Potter, Martin (Gary Oldman) has grown tired of being a grown-up and yearns to return to a childhood he feels he has missed. One can sense the same instinct at work in Chaplin's Tramp as he vacillates between the impulse to be a child pretending to be an adult or an adult pretending to be a child. To phrase it somewhat differently, an artist's fascination with childhood might reflect his reluctance to enter an adult society from which he feels alienated. The two prototypes of this kind of personality in literature would be Lewis Carroll and J. M. Barrie, whose *Alice in Wonderland* and *Peter Pan*, respectively, are probably still the touchstones of imaginative/fantasy literature about the world of childhood. In Gavin Millar's *Dreamchild* (1985), again scripted by Dennis Potter, scenes from the life of Charles Dodgson (Ian Holm) are intercut with parallel events from Lewis Carroll's fantasy viewed from a twentieth-century perspective, as a now eighty-year-old Alice Liddell reflects on the work she inspired and the man who endured her thoughtless childhood cruelty and continued to adore her. 'At the time I was too young to see the gift whole', she says in a final speech, 'to see it for what it was and to acknowledge the love that had given it birth. I see it now at long, long last. Thank you, Mr Dodgson. Thank you.'

The modern cinematic equivalent to Carroll and Barrie would be filmland's Peter Pan and wunderkind, Steven Spielberg, who became a father himself at the age of 40 before he made a film about a particularly brutal ending of childhood, *Empire of the Sun* (1987). Yet if an artist seems often reluctant to leave the world of childhood, it might not be a sign of immaturity so much as a recognition of a certain kinship between the artist and the child. If artists are drawn to childhood, might the reason be that they see in the child something of their own feelings of isolation, insecurity, self-absorption, and the fear and excitement of endeavouring to confront and create a new world? Might the fascination, for artist and audience, also stem from the fact that childhood might contain the clue that explains not only why that person has become an artist but also the kind of artist that person has become? Literary classics like James Joyce's *A Portrait of the Artist as a Young Man*, D. H. Lawrence's *Sons and Lovers* and Thomas Mann's *Tonio Kröger*, have traditionally invited readings along those lines. A similar approach could be adopted to cinematic masterpieces like Andrei Tarkovsky's *Mirror* (1975) and Louis Malle's *Au Revoir, les Enfants* (1987).

The artist looking back to his own childhood as a clue to his modern existence is all part of an endless attempt, on all our behalfs, to rewrite and analyse our own history. It contrasts with a more traditional, more sentimental usage of children in drama, whereby they are offered as a

Victorian childhood: croquet on the lawn in *Dreamchild* (1985)

symbol of the future and the hope of forthcoming generations. Even westerns as different as John Ford's *Stagecoach* (1939), in which the Indian is represented as the main agent of danger and chaos, and Robert Aldrich's *Apache* (1954), in which an Indian is the persecuted hero, both use the sound of a baby's cry to suggest new possibilities for their respective societies: new civilization in the wilderness, the possibility of future harmony and reconciliation between races. George Stevens' modern western *Giant* (1956) closes on a huge close-up of the Benedicts' grandchildren, who represent the hope for racial integration in America's future. The classic western – pre-eminently George Stevens' *Shane* (1953) – was very careful in the way it used children as a means of interpreting the legacy of the West correctly: appreciating the courage and heroism of the pioneers, yet subsuming their legacy of violence under a new, more peaceful civilization. Because of this, Sam Peckinpah's use of children in westerns like *The Wild Bunch* (1969) and

9

Pat Garrett and Billy the Kid (1973) came as a considerable shock, for he showed the West's violent legacy not as being understood and rejected by the succeeding young generation but assimilated and even imitated.

Peckinpah's view of children in his westerns belongs to what one might call a modernist pessimism about the transition from nineteenth- to twentieth-century civilization. Henry James called the First World War a 'plunge of civilization into this abyss of blood and darkness' and felt a shiver of premonition of what it might portend for the new age. Indeed, ever since little Father Time in Thomas Hardy's *Jude the Obscure* killed two children and then himself 'becos we are too menny ...' in a gesture that was to be characterized as part of the 'future universal wish not to live ...', modern artists have found it harder to use children as glib pointers to a brave new world. In a century that has already seen two world wars, death camps on an almost unimaginable scale and the paralysing prospect of global annihilation, the future itself as an optimistic concept has been devalued. The modern artist has been much more tempted to use the plight of children to exemplify the sorry condition of contemporary civilization. *Empire of the Sun* is relevant here, for it shows the impact on a child's sensibility not only of global warfare but also of the first atomic explosion: suddenly the stakes are not victory or defeat, but the survival or annihilation of the future. Soviet film-makers, such as Andrei Tarkovsky in *The Sacrifice* (1985) and Konstantin Lopushansky in *Letters from a Dead Man* (1985) have been particularly sensitive to the status and symbolic significance of childhood in a nuclear age. Made shortly before Chernobyl, Lopushansky's film has disturbing visions of irradiated orphans in a state of shock and of a nightmarish visit to a children's hospital ward. It concludes with images of children as they struggle across a frozen landscape to an uncertain future. Reflecting on the legacy left by his generation, a father writes to his son: 'People say that children enjoy discovering the world, but even in good times children are fearful ...'

Not surprisingly, given the range of resonances childhood as a theme evokes amongst artists, a number of traditions and conventions have developed in their manner of depiction. From writers like Mark Twain, Nathaniel Hawthorne and Henry James has developed the tradition of the 'wise child', who has an innate wisdom and a sharp, sometimes alarmingly keen and accurate perception that can disconcert adults. In literature two distinguished examples of this kind of characterization would be Pearl in Hawthorne's *The Scarlet Letter*, with her preternatural insight into her mother's and Dimmesdale's hearts, and Maisie in James's *What Maisie Knew*, with her incisive idealism in a world of corruption and deceit. Alas, in the cinema this conception has been too often corrupted. Percipience has been transformed into sentimental precociousness, whereby a Shirley Temple, a Hayley Mills, a Little Lord Fauntleroy or a troupe of Trapps can contrive to melt the heart of a gruff elder with their unexpected warm humanity. Alternatively, it has been made into a vehicle of horror as exemplified by the little girl Mary (Karen Balkin) in William Wyler's film version of Lillian Hellman's *The Children's Hour* (1961) who, because she does not like them, accuses her teachers (Audrey Hepburn and Shirley MacLaine) of having a lesbian relationship. When the teachers protest their

The wicked very young: Mary (Karen Balkin, left) torments Rosalie (Veronica Cartwright, right) in *The Children's Hour* (UK title: *The Loudest Whisper*), in William Wyler's 1961 version of the Lillian Hellman play

innocence, the grandmother (Fay Bainter) says: 'How could a child her age *know* of such things? She could scarcely make them up!' In fact, children of her age – like the girl in *The Bad Seed* (1956) or the boy in *The Omen* (1976) – might 'know' of such things either out of their own evil or through their being impregnated, as it were, by the corruption and horror of the adult world. In a crude way, what is at stake here is often the whole notion of the innate innocence of childhood.

It is only to be expected, of course, that the depiction of childhood in cinema contains some of the same limitations of cinema itself as an institution. For example, the over-emphasis on male children, which the selection for this book inevitably and sadly reflects, is an aspect of the cinema's being throughout its history an essentially male-dominated industry. Also, and this is equally true of other artistic forms, the cinema's depiction of childhood has been an essentially *adult* construction. In depicting childhood, the cinema – and this is no less true of the book industry – has generally excluded, creatively speaking, the voice that could

The death of a child as punishment for adult transgression: from *Mildred Pierce* (1945). Joan Crawford as Mildred (centre); on her left are Ann Blyth as her spoilt elder daughter and Mannart Kippen as the doctor; on her right, Bruce Bennett as her husband

speak with first-hand authority on the subject: namely, the child him/herself. Hardly any films have been made *by* children *for* children: it is the reason that so many films about childhood turn out to be essentially about something else – the past, memory, nostalgia, lost innocence. Indeed, practitioners who have specialized in films *for* children (the complex case of Disney is the most prominent example, though one could also include Colin Finbow's esteemed Children's Film Unit) have either seen their products marginalized into matinée rather than mainstream programming, or have presented a saccharine image that not even children themselves can stomach. It might be, for example, that monster Freddie Krueger's enormous popularity amongst kids in the *Nightmare on Elm Street* series of films is because, at last, someone is killing off those appalling American screen brats that audiences have had to put up with for so long.

The main problem with children in films has always been the problem of sentimentality, though perhaps Charles Dickens was the first and biggest culprit in this regard. 'Only a heart of stone could read the death of Little Nell without laughing', said Oscar Wilde of *The Old Curiosity Shop*, and the predictable, anticipated death of a child has been handled with Victorian excess in David Selznick's emotional piledriver *Gone With The Wind* (1939) and even in Stanley Kubrick's epic of detachment, *Barry Lyndon* (1975). On the whole, though, the shock and emotional devastation of the death of a child has been treated with great authenticity, integrity and power in film thrillers such as Alfred Hitchcock's *Sabotage* (1936), Claude Chabrol's *Killer* (1969), and Nicolas Roeg's *Don't Look Now* (1973). Films like Luchino Visconti's *L'Innocente* (1976) and Colin Gregg's *Lamb* (1987) use the death of a child as an effective dramatic event to highlight the appalling conse-quences of adult selfishness and lack of self-knowledge. Although perhaps not touching the profundity of artistic expression in, for example, Gustav Mahler's desolate song cycle *Kindertotenlieder* or Jon Silkin's eloquent poetic lament 'Death of a Son' or James Agee's autobiographical novel, *A Death in the Family*, film melodramas like George Stevens's *Penny Serenade* (1941), Michael Curtiz's *Mildred Pierce* (1945) and Martin Ritt's *Pete 'n' Tillie* (1972) very effectively show the traumatic effect such a tragedy has on the parents, in which guilt seems to weigh almost as strongly as grief. More dubious has been the use of children as a kind of moral blackmail, a charge that could be levelled at films as distinguished as *Bicycle Thieves* (1948) or *Salaam Bombay* (1988) as well as at more obvious targets like *The Sound of Music* (1965). When the plight of children is highlighted in films like these, one is reminded a little of the conflicting emotions induced by 'Children in Need' telethons: namely, that vital questions about a society's inability or even unwillingness to provide adequate resources for such sufferers are being subsumed under an orgy of self-congratulating compassion and charity; and that what is needed is not an annual sentimental gala to tap society's heart but a *regular*, rigorous analysis of that society to show where it is going wrong.

Sentimentality has not always been the response of the artist to children. The attitude of some artists to children is a revelation of their misanthropy, classically so in the case of W. C. Fields, to whom children were an unmitigated pest; but also in the cynical worlds of Claude Chabrol and Alfred Hitchcock (notice how often they bring down the former's bourgeois world, or with what relish, for example, Robert Walker even pauses on his way to murder in Hitchcock's 1951 movie *Strangers on a Train* to pop a child's balloon). Yet there are directors who have shown a particular affinity with and sensitivity to the world of childhood: Jack Clayton, Alexander Mackendrick and Carol Reed in Great Britain, George Stevens and Steven Spielberg in America, and, on the international scene, Bergman, Tarkovsky and, in particular, François Truffaut.

Representative films by the above directors have more or less selected themselves for inclusion. Elsewhere, candidacy for inclusion has been affected by decisions, (a) to concentrate on the post-war era, making exceptions only for Chaplin's *The Kid* (1921) and Minnelli's *Meet Me in St Louis* (1944), which seemed to demand inclusion; (b) to take the age of 13 as a nominal cut off point for childhood; (c) to forego a survey of child stars, which has been done elsewhere and which is really outside the concern of this book; and (d) to organize the material mainly under thematic headings, which in some chapters makes for a rather unexpected and unusual

13

The street children in
Mira Nair's *Salaam
Bombay* (1988)

conjunction of movies but also graphically demonstrates how the theme of childhood has persistently cut across period, genre and nationality. Pulsing through the text are a cluster of recurrent questions or debates. How has the point of view of the child been represented, *visually* as well as thematically? Should fiction about childhood and/or for children be predominantly in the mode of fantasy (idealistic, 'improving' texts that appeal to the imagination) or realism (texts that prepare children for the complexities of adult life)? For whom are films about childhood made, and what meaning have film artists drawn from their explorations of childhood experience? Perhaps the largest question is this: if the attitude to children, in art and in life, reflects the health or sickness of civilization, what do such films reveal about our condition? In this regard, the book might not make reassuring reading, but it is to be hoped that it will be a thought-provoking experience.

CHAPTER ONE

DREAMS OF ADVENTURE

---

*The authors of genuine children's literature
are only rarely and indirectly educators.
They are poets whose imagination is
privileged to remain on the dream
wavelength of childhood.*

(ANDRÉ BAZIN, *What is Cinema? Volume 1*)

*People should always believe in kids – they
should even believe their lies.*

(MR ZABLADOWSKY in *The 5,000 Fingers of Dr T*)

THE most popular film genre for children is the fantasy or adventure film, in most examples of which children have themselves a role to play, either as observers or participants. The industry assumes that children prefer action and excitement to anything contemplative and therefore offers a narrative that has something of the child's own energy and vitality, being mindful also of the changing tastes of children from generation to generation.

Actually, in recent years, what children have often been given is ancient fare dressed up in modern costume. What has been involved has not been an act of imagination so much as a time-transplant. Robert Louis Stevenson's *Treasure Island* gets a different outing in Richard Donner's *The Goonies* (1985), an incongruously modern tale of piracy and buried treasure. H. G. Wells's *The Time Machine* is given a new twist by the time-travelling pyrotechnics of Terry Gilliam's *Time Bandits* (1982) and by Robert Zemeckis's *Back to the Future* (1985), which implies that a sense of history is so little ingrained in American youth that it would not even recognize an era as recent as the 1950s. The Flash Gordon series and the traditional goodies-versus-baddies western are re-decorated with modern technology in George Lucas's *Star Wars* (1977).

There is a peculiar dichotomy at the heart of such films. Professing to appeal to the superior imagination of the child before maturity dulls his or

Childhood as adventure: Simon Harrison (left), Candice Bergen (centre) and Polly Gottesman (right) as the besieged American family in *The Wind and the Lion* (1975)

her sense of fantasy, films often seem to prefer formula to freshness and lazily duplicate traditional structures. They also offer an adult perception of what children are supposed to enjoy, with the result that the film-maker becomes less of an imaginative creator than a toy manufacturer (a situation that George Lucas has embraced). The new children's film, then, too often creates a desire but does not satisfy a need. Screenwriter William Goldman has made a distinction between the older type of kids' film, like *Bambi* (1942), which an adult can still watch with pleasure and recall what excited him or her about it as a child, and the newer type of kids' film like *Star Wars*, where the adult response is more likely to be sheepish embarrassment at ever being seduced by something so facile even as an infant.

What, then, is the ideal fantasy film for children? The archetype is still probably *The Wizard of Oz* (1939), which remains the cinema's nearest equivalent to *Alice in Wonderland*. One of its strengths is its recognition of something that acute artistic observers of childhood, from Dickens to Disney, have always sensed: that it is often more effective to appeal to a child's sense of fear than to his or her sense of fun. So much of a child's life can be spent in a state of apprehensive anticipation that a narrative structured like a nightmare from which one can emerge unscathed might be a genuinely cathartic experience. Early Disney, like *Snow White and the Seven Dwarfs* (1937) and *Pinocchio* (1940) certainly exploited the element of terror, and the spookiness of *The Wizard of Oz*, which, as Graham Greene noted at the time, prompted the British Board of Film Censors to give it a certificate for adults only on its first release, is undoubtedly an indispensable part of its charm for children.

Then there is its dream structure. As shrewdly noted in the André Bazin epigraph that heads this chapter, many of the best examples of children's fiction have the atmosphere of dream, as if this is the principal means whereby the artist can re-enter the world of childhood and the realm of pure imagination. Great literature, for and about childhood, often concerns the transforming power of the imagination, which is a crucial aspect of the resilience of the children and where danger, and even horror, can be transmuted into story-book adventure. J. G. Ballard's novel *Empire of the Sun* has that quality, and so too does Richard Hughes's novel about children kidnapped by pirates, *A High Wind in Jamaica*, memorably filmed by Alexander Mackendrick in 1965. John Milius's admiration for that film shows up in his epic adventure-cum-political satire, *The Wind and the Lion* (1975): indeed, as a mini-tribute to *Jamaica*, he casts the actress who played the young heroine in Mackendrick's film, Deborah Baxter, in a small guest role. In Milius's film, two children, kidnapped as pawns in a political game, turn their dangerous situation into one of escapist excitement. The slow-motion shot of Sean Connery's Arab brigand as he rides towards the boy for the last time is one of the cinema's most awesome images of romanticism and hero worship, crystallizing the impact on the boy of his captor's bravado and the young lad's swelling sense of having been part of a wonderful adventure.

Yet sometimes the imagination acts not so much as a transformation of reality as a significantly distorted comment on it. In *The Wizard of Oz*, for example, people from Dorothy's actual Kansas world are transformed into

Classic fantasy: *The Wizard of Oz* (1939). Dorothy (Judy Garland) is amazed by her strange new companions, Scarecrow (Ray Bolger, left), Cowardly Lion (Bert Lahr, centre) and Tin Man (Jack Haley, right)

fanciful shapes in her dream that might represent the fears and desires of her subconscious. Her querulous and hated neighbour, who complains about Dorothy's dog, turns up in the dream as the Wicked Witch who must be destroyed. *The 5,000 Fingers of Dr T* (1953) does similar things with its characters, whilst in Richard Franklin's *Cloak and Dagger* (1984) a young boy's fantasy life is also intimately linked to his real world, notably in his conferring a heroic image in his fantasy on the features of his father who, by implication, has thus far not lived up to expectations. Something like that is also implicit in the dreamlike quality of *Shane* (1953), as if Shane materializes out of the boy's subconscious in answer to a need for a heroism that his decent, mundane father cannot provide.

This is another dimension that *The Wizard of Oz* acknowledges: namely, that the form a child's escapism takes might be revealing about the world in which the child habitually lives. Most adventure in children's fiction takes place outside the immediate family context, where the parents are either

19

absent, or not in the know, or changed into different, sometimes unflattering roles. Might this imply a dissatisfaction with the family structure, which, by its very nature, seems to deny the opportunity for adventure and excitement? Yet the implicit subversiveness of this theme not only rarely finds expression but also is commonly reversed by the end of the film, as if the adventure has been a sort of temporary aberration and the child returns gratefully to the family womb. Dorothy in *Oz* concludes that there is no place like home, and Elliott in *E.T.* returns with tearful satisfaction to a family, none of whose problems have really been resolved. At the end of *The Goonies*, the children ride to the rescue of their parents' suburban homes (which have been threatened by property developers), seemingly forgetting that it has been their dissatisfaction with ineffectual parents and their frustration with boring suburbia that have precipitated their desire for excitement in the first place. Only Joe Dante, in films like *Gremlins* (1984) and *Explorers* (1985), carries through an anarchic attitude to suburbia (or Spielbergia), which strikes one as a more authentic dramatiz-

A child to lift America out of her Depression: Aileen Quinn (left) in the title role of John Huston's only musical, *Annie (1982)*. With Ann Reinking (right)

ation of children's attitudes. The thematic conservatism of some of the other films reinforces the idea that what we are being given is an *adult* perspective on childhood, and wish-fulfilment fantasies that might actually have more relevance to older rather than younger people.

It might be a recognition of this duality – the contradictions and tensions that emerge from a 'children's cinema' that is constructed by adults – that has partially prompted the recent spate of generation-reversal comedies such as Penny Marshall's *Big* (1988), Brian Gilbert's *Vice-Versa* (1988) and Rod Daniel's *Like Father, Like Son* (1988), in which parents and children, by various narrative strategies, are obliged to swap roles for a while and feel what life is like in the other's shoes. A feminine version of the trend had been anticipated in the unusually excellent Disney comedy *Freaky Friday* (1976), scripted by Mary Rodgers and directed by Gary Nelson, in which mother Barbara Harris and daughter Jodie Foster change personalities for a day. The purpose of these films is overt comedy: a new slant on sibling rivalry in *Freaky Friday*; adults behaving like daft kids in *Big* and kids becoming even more insufferably precocious than usual in *Vice-Versa* (says a taxi-driver about the young lad who is now behaving with the yuppie insolence of his father: 'That boy's gonna be famous – I'm gonna kill him'). But perhaps there could be a lurking seriousness behind the humour. As Penny Marshall expressed it in her production notes for *Big*: 'The story is how a child's innocence can touch people and make them realise certain things about themselves that, getting caught up in the rat race of life, they forget.' Even if the movie does not live up to it, it is a nice thought.

THE 5,000 FINGERS OF DR T

(USA 1953: Roy Rowland)

This is one of the most unusual and attractive fantasies in Hollywood cinema. A young boy, Bartholomew Collins (Tommy Rettig) hates his piano lessons and would rather be playing baseball. He is berated by his fearsome piano teacher, Mr Terwilliker (Hans Conried); exhorted to practise by his widowed mother (Mary Healy); and given no comfort by the family plumber, Mr Zabladowsky (Peter Lind Hayes). Slowly, as in *The Wizard of Oz*, all these characters from Bart's 'real' world are to be transformed into different roles when he drifts into a dream. Dr T becomes an evil genius who has enticed away five hundred children to perform his new compositional masterpiece on a giant two-layered piano. Bart's mother is now Dr T's secretary, and in hypnotic thrall to her master. Having come to install 500 sinks for the boys, Mr Zabladowsky is at first sceptical of Bart's story of imprisonment but is convinced when Bart finds a decree from Dr T that the plumber should be 'disintegrated'.

Co-written by Allan Scott, who has co-authored a number of classic Astaire-Rogers musicals, including *Top Hat* (1935) and *Swing Time* (1936), the script is mainly the brainchild of Dr Seuss (Theodore Geisel), who had scripted the famous UPA cartoon, *Gerald McBoing Boing* (1952) and was the author and illustrator of numerous children's books. Apparently, the inspiration for the film came from the memory of his own childhood piano lessons and the sadism of his teacher, who would rap his knuckles with a pencil whenever he made a mistake. The film is a revenge on this teacher, but interestingly takes some care to present the whole action and experience through the boy's eyes. Bart is present in every scene and the spectacle has a stark simplicity and economy that convincingly reflects a child's uncluttered vision. Everything, from costumes to characters, is quite bizarre: uneven staircases, blue and pink architecture, caps with fingers on them, twin skaters united by a single beard, and a bedroom for Dr T that has a metronome for a clock.

The dream structure seems one of the easiest and most effective ways of entering a child's imagination. It is a structure that allows a creative artist to roam freely in a child's subconscious and throw up some interesting sub-themes that could not emerge within a more naturalistic drama. For example, without spelling it out too explicitly, the dream basically expresses Bart's unconscious fear that his mother, sufficiently transformed into a beautiful woman, could become Dr T's wife. The fantasy is a projection of his anxiety about the vulnerability of his widowed mother, the rivalry for her between him and a future father figure (nightmarishly embodied by Dr T), and the search for a new father, which is where the plumber comes in. If all this sounds more like *Hamlet* than children's fantasy, it should be noted that Dr T does quote from *Hamlet* at one stage in the film and that, for example, the twins are as inseparable as Rosencrantz and Guildenstern.

The dream also takes the form of a fantasy about adult discipline being routed by childish anarchy. What is curious about this sub-theme is the imagery used to enforce it. Adult discipline is likened to Fascism, with Dr T as a great dictator as well as conductor. Childish anarchy is represented in the form of atomic energy, which demolishes Dr T's Metropolis. It is a curiously ferocious metaphor, but it does express the intensity of the frustration felt by children at the tyranny of their elders and the inability of adults to enter into their childish fantasy world. 'People should always believe in kids,' says Zabladowsky, 'they should even believe their lies.' It is a theme that, as we shall see, is prominent in many children's films, from *The Curse of the Cat People* (1944) to *The Snowman* (1982): the difference between 'untruth' and 'acceptable fantasy' and the difficulty children have in making themselves believed. The artistic trick is to fix on a detail that gives validity to the fantasy without undermining the quality of dream. In *The Snowman* the bridge between the world of fantasy and reality is a scarf that has been given to the boy by Father Christmas and which at the end he finds in his pocket. In *Dr T* it is a plaster on the plumber's thumb: in 'real' life, he cannot recall how it got there, but it relates to a moment in the dream section of the narrative when he and Bart made a blood pact.

More than the fantasy, or Frederick Hollander's brilliant score, or Hans Conried's best-ever screen performance as Dr T (unless one includes his superb vocal characterization of Captain Hook in Disney's *Peter Pan*), it is the film's capacity for empathizing with a child's world and emotions that is its most attractive characteristic. There are some clever games with genre, as it duplicates the anti-intellectualism of the traditional musical (baseball preferable to Beethoven) and sends up the sci-fi films of the 1950s; and there is a wonderful variation on a young person's guide to the orchestra, where Bart wanders into Dr T's dungeons for non-piano players and sets off a

The concert in
The 5,000 Fingers of Dr T
(1953)

performance for piccolos, trombones, xylophones, horns and accordions, building to a surreal climax with a huge harp and with the bodies of violins seeming more like mannequins than musical instruments. Nevertheless, the most poignant musical moment is Bart's solo, a song of lament, 'Just because we're kids . . . Just because you wear a wallet near your heart', he sings, 'You think you're smart/I'd hate to grow/Like some I know/Who like to push us little kids around.' Not many numbers in musicals convey so sensitively and unsentimentally what it feels like to be a child in a grown-up's world.

SHANE

(USA 1953: George Stevens)

'The attention of everyone in the room, like a single sense, was centred on that dark figure just inside the swinging doors, back to them and touching them. This was the Shane of the adventures I had dreamed for him, cool and competent, facing that room full of men in the simple solitude of his own invincible completeness.'[1] So says the boy narrator of Jack Schaefer's novel, *Shane*, as the eponymous hero moves into the saloon for the final gunfight that will cleanse the valley of evil. The heightened prose reflects the mythic dimensions of the theme, with Shane, as a knight in shining buckskin, as saviour of the range. The child's perspective intensifies and validates the idealization of the hero and the polarity of the conflict between good and evil. A hint is planted also that the tale is essentially a boy's dream of stirring and impossible adventure and of larger than life characters: ('This was the Shane of the adventures I had dreamed for him . . .').

Mercifully avoiding the pomposity of the novel's language and the narcissism of its hero, the film nevertheless shrewdly retains its most significant narrative feature, namely, its concentration on the point of view of the little boy, Joey (Brandon de Wilde), who develops a crush on Shane (Alan Ladd), even saying his name as if it were a form of caress. Joey (called 'Bob' in the novel) is the first to see Shane arrive in the valley and the last to see him leave, and throughout seems to follow enviously in his shadow, imitating his walk and on hand to watch his most stirring encounters – the first fight with Calloway (Ben Johnson) in the saloon, the final gunfight with Wilson (Jack Palance).

Is *Shane* then, just a little boy's view of the ideal western hero? Not quite, because although Joey is the film's principal observer, director George Stevens plays interestingly in the margins of those incidents that Joey either does not see, or sees but does not fully understand. By focusing on the boy's point of view, the director can play up the stylization of the characterization and treatment, transforming his simple western tale into the stuff of Arthurian legend. Shane and Wilson come to stand for Good and Evil; there are Shakespearian convulsions in nature to intensify dramatic highpoints; and Victor Young's noble score seems in places a conscious homage to Walton's Agincourt music for *Henry V* (1944). At the same time, however, Stevens modifies and complicates the tone of reverie and nostalgia in certain places where Joey's perception is absent or defective.

For example, Joey is not present during the scene when Wilson guns down one of the farmers, Torrey (Elisha Cook Jr), in the street. Joey's absence is the cue for Stevens to treat the scene with unusual violence (the impact of the shot will knock Torrey flat on his back and send him slithering in the mud), and imply the negative side of Joey's fascination with Shane's gun, which he sees as symbolic of his hero's power. 'A gun is a tool, Marian', Shane explains to Joey's mother, 'as good or bad as the man using it'; but Marian (Jean Arthur) insists that 'guns aren't going to be my boy's life' and comments that everyone would be better off if there were no more guns in the valley, including Shane's.

This touches on one of the most powerful unspoken areas of the film: the impact of Shane, and Joey's hero-worship of him, on Joey's mother. Shane is the man Joey would like to become in his wildest dreams – but where does this leave Joey's father (Van Heflin), and is Joey's day-dreaming triggering a yearning in Marian too? 'Joey, don't get to liking Shane too much', says Marian, 'because some day he'll have to go away and you'll be upset.' It seems sound advice to protect the child's feelings, yet it might also be intended to protect the image in Joey's eyes of her husband who seems to be diminishing a little in comparison. More pointedly, it might actually be a warning to herself not to grow too fond of Shane: this is beautifully conveyed by Stevens and Jean Arthur in a tiny gesture – the quick way she blows out the boy's lamp, before he can notice the slight embarrassment on her face and self-consciousness in her voice. This is one of those key moments whose full significance Joey does not see.

There are two other scenes involving his mother and Shane, the full significance of which Joey cannot grasp. When Joey asks Shane to stay his appeal is interrupted by his mother's call to breakfast, and the camera lingers momentarily on the hero: the implication is that it is the sound of *Marian's* voice, not Joey's, that is the significant factor in Shane's changing his mind. Later, after the epic fight between Shane and Joey's father to stop the latter's going into town to confront Wilson ('Could you whip 'im, Pa? Could you whip Shane?' Joey has asked earlier, as if prophesying the confrontation), Joey has berated Shane for his actions – 'You hit him with your gun, I hate you' – and it is Joey's mother who has to interpret what Shane has done. In their farewell scene, Marian and Shane seem nearly on the point of declaring their feelings but, in a neat reversal of the earlier scene when it is Marian's voice that has most influenced the course of the scene, now it is Joey's. 'Mother . . .' he calls softly, calling Marian back to her role in the family. Nevertheless, in the master stroke of the echoing hills at the end of the film, when Joey is calling after the departing Shane, it is striking that the echo starts on the line: 'And mother wants you . . . wants you . . . I know she does . . . she does . . .'. The scene is so moving because Joey, unwittingly, might be articulating his mother's pain of separation as well as his own.

Elsewhere in the film, Stevens uses children more conventionally, though entirely without cuteness. Something of the director's experience in silent comedy, filming Laurel and Hardy shorts, is evident in the bar-room brawl, where a blow from Shane is visually matched to a shot of Joey's taking a convulsive bite from his stick of candy (it is a moment that is an amusing echo of Joey's earlier revelation about what had happened to a former employee of his father in Shane's situation: 'They knocked his teeth out!'). As well as comedy, children are used for purposes of counterpoint, very beautifully in the scene at Torrey's funeral (later Shane will offer the children as the reason the farmers ought to stay and fight) and remarkably in a moment of uncomfortable innocence when Torrey's body is being carried past the homesteaders and one of the small girls starts waving at it. Arthur Penn would enlarge on that kind of incongruity in a famous moment from *The Left-Handed Gun* (1958) when a sheriff is blasted out of his boots and a child laughs at the curious comedy of the image, a laughter promptly cut short when his mother slaps him across the face.

Perhaps more than any other film of this genre, *Shane* comprehensively expresses the role of children in westerns. Through the examples set by their elders, children learn the values that will enable them to take their place in society: and in this regard Joey has an unrivalled set of tutors. The actions of children remind us of the aggression we are all born with and have either to restrain or channel constructively. In *Shane* this is particularly

indicated in Joey's fascination with Shane's gun and his own toy rifle: it is as a hunter that we first see him. Significantly, though, his final game with his gun – rampaging round the house, shouting 'Bang! Bang!' whilst his father is readying himself for a confrontation that could end in his death – takes his mother to the point of near-breakdown. Her fear has been that, particularly through Shane's example, Joey might be contaminated by the frontier myth and the instinct for violence that seems to accompany it. (Shane's own contamination by it is vividly demonstrated in the film's early part: his lightning reactions towards his gun twice make Joey jump out of his skin.) This later theme will become a major preoccupation of Sam Peckinpah in films like *The Wild Bunch* (1969), in which children are woven into the whole fabric of violence and eventually, inevitably, become participators. In *Shane*, however, Joey remains an observer and Shane's final gunfight will serve not as an example but as an exorcism. With his final gesture of placing his hand on Joey's head, as if anointing him for the future, this most ethereal of action heroes sanctifies and civilizes little Joey before riding on; and the cinema's most potent study of childlike hero-worship closes within a dream.

THE RED BALLOON
(France 1956: Albert Lamorisse)

The Red Balloon is a fantasy short film about a little boy (Pascal Lamorisse) who is followed through the Paris streets by a red balloon, which consequently becomes his inseparable companion. Because of this he incurs the jealousy of other schoolchildren who pursue him and ultimately burst his balloon. At this point a multitude of multi-coloured balloons from all corners of Paris converge towards the distraught lad, lifting him off the ground as he catches hold of their strings and carrying him towards the heavens.

Although other Lamorisse films, such as *Crin Blanc – White Stallion* (1952) and *Stowaway in the Sky* (1960), have also evoked the fantasy and wonder of a child's world, *The Red Balloon* is undoubtedly his most famous and popular film, even winning the original screenplay Oscar against such powerful competition as the Ealing classic *The Ladykillers* (1955) and Federico Fellini's *La Strada* (1954). Yet over the years the film has generated a certain amount of controversy, rather surprisingly for such a trifle. Some find it charming, others calculating and condescending. Also there have been heated disagreements over aspects of its style and theme. Childhood remains one of the most contentious of screen subjects, even when as here it is given one of its most ostensibly innocuous expressions.

It is a simple and pretty film, exquisitely photographed by Edmond Sechan and lyrically scored by Maurice LeRoux. Most commentators would agree on that. Yet even André Bazin, who admired the film, thought that its theme might be a little too intellectual and thus dispel a little of its childlike quality. The theme, presumably, is intended as an allegory of Good and Evil, in which Evil wins on Earth, but Good transcends reality and soars to a higher realm. In this regard, it becomes almost a religious movie.

The style is what Bazin characterized as 'imaginative documentary' – the kind of poetic realism that Robert Flaherty brought to his documentary

School of violence: Shane (Alan Ladd) teaches Joey (Brandon De Wilde) how to shoot in *Shane* (1953)

about childhood, *Louisiana Story* (1948). In one sense it is clearly fantastic and faked. The balloon was apparently controlled by an imperceptible nylon thread handled by Lamorisse. Far from their being just one red balloon, half a million francs of the budget was spent on purchasing a massive supply of alternatives to act as screen doubles. Nevertheless, Lamorisse has gone to great lengths to give the action as much authenticity as possible. This not only means shooting on location, but also relying as little as possible on montage trickery. By showing the boy and balloon in the same shot, the film is given a sense of spacial reality and the story an appearance of a real event unfolding naturally rather than a gimmicky situation artificially hyped by special effects and trick editing.

Nevertheless, François Truffaut felt that this scrupulous attention to realism only emphasized the artificiality and sentimentality of the whole concept. The balloon is insufferably cute, like a bad child actor, and its anthropomorphic antics are no better than those to which critics were beginning to object in the wildlife documentaries of Walt Disney. It also acts more like a servant than a friend to the little boy and its fate at the hands of the other urchins is mere melodramatic contrivance. We never gain any insight into the character of the little boy, says Truffaut. There is no poetry nor imagination in his presentation. We are merely invited to find him lovable because he is persecuted by some psychological bullies. Only in the final moments, as the coloured balloons soar over the grey roofs (colour standing for imagination, grey for mundane reality) does the film attain any kind of imaginative stature or symbolic piquancy.

I must say I am more on the side of Truffaut than of the film's admirers: the balloon has always seemed to me more lead than red, yet there is a certain irony about Truffaut's malicious little satire on the Lamorisse formula of film-making that concludes his review: 'All it takes is to oppose a nice little boy against a few villains with, as the object of conflict, an appealing little animal or a pretty little "something".'[2] It is designed to show how facile the formula is, but a quarter of a century later in a supposedly more sophisticated age, that formula was to be appropriated wholesale and fashioned into the biggest commercial success in film history. The main difference was that the 'pretty little "something"' was to be an extra-terrestrial whom, as Steven Spielberg was to say, 'only a mother could love'.

THE BLACK STALLION
(USA 1979: Carroll Ballard)

'From the moment he first saw the stallion, he knew it would either destroy him, or carry him where no one had ever been before. . . .' So reads the film poster from *The Black Stallion*, based on Walter Farley's classic children's novel published in 1941. It tells the story of the bond that grows between a stallion and a young boy, Alec Ramsey (Kelly Reno), when they are marooned together on a desert island. When the boy is rescued he insists on returning to his home in America with the stallion. He meets a former racehorse trainer and jockey, Henry (Mickey Rooney), and under his guidance, rides the stallion to victory in a race specially staged to find the fastest horse in the country.

David Shipman has called the movie 'the best children's film since *The*

A passion for animals is a familiar theme in children's stories and this is one of the most famous examples: Elizabeth Taylor and horse in *National Velvet* (1945)

Wizard of Oz'[3], but one suspects that producer Francis Ford Coppola's intentions were even more ambitious than that. Later to be followed by his stylish and visually elaborate adaptations of S. E. Hinton's *The Outsiders* (1983) and *Rumble Fish* (1983), *The Black Stallion* was probably his first attempt at establishing a new sub-genre: 'art movies' for kids. The artiness of the movie manifests itself in a number of ways. Although the work of three very capable hands, namely Melissa Mathison (who was to write *E.T.*), Jeanne Rosenberg (author of the superb screenplay for Disney's *The Journey of Natty Gann* (1985)) and William D. Witliff (writer of *Raggedy Man* (1981), *Barbarossa* (1984) and *Country* (1985)), the screenplay is remarkably clipped, functional, oblique and understated. The visual style is consistently incisive and surprising, with none of the comfortable middle-distance shooting that contributes to the cosy atmosphere of the conventional family film. Finally, the movie is full of erudite literary and classical allusions. Unfortunately, underlying the whole concept is a familiar child/animal formula that has been typical of the children's film from *Lassie Come Home* (1943) to *Old Yeller* (1957), and however you try to beef it up artistically – and John Steinbeck's *The Red Pony* tries very hard – it is almost impossible to defeat the twin problems of sentimentality and predictability. *The Black Stallion* clears the first hurdle very well, but falters at the second.

The opening scenes on board ship are sharply observed. The relationship between boy and stallion is swiftly established: the boy's sympathy for the animal's ill treatment, the stallion's reciprocal alertness to the boy's safety. When it whinnies as Alec is giving it sugar cubes, it seems as if the boy has startled it but it is actually a warning – the Arab owner has stolen up behind the boy to punish him. At this point the larger dimensions of the theme are foreshadowed. Triggered by his winning of a small bronze horse amongst other trinkets in a card game, Alec's father (Hoyt Axton) tells the boy the story of Alexander the Great's magic horse, Bucephalus, whom the young Alexander had claimed as his own when he proved he could ride it. 'He was just about your size, just about your age', says his father to Alec. Just as King Philip had made a gift of the horse to Alexander, so the bronze horse is a gift to Alec from his father, and when the father dies in the shipwreck, the bronze horse will come to life in the form of the stallion.

'I was in the water, I couldn't breathe . . . I called out for Dad', says Alec when telling his mother (Teri Garr) about the shipwreck and about how the stallion had saved his life. The father's description of Bucephalus – 'smoke coming out of his nose . . . fire in his eyes . . .' – that so amuses Alec is actually a premonition of the fire and smoke that are shortly to engulf them, and indeed the first sign that something is wrong occurs when the bronze horse topples from a shelf as if in warning. Apart from a suspicion of racial stereotyping in the supporting characterization (the shifty Arab, the mercenary Jew, etc.), this opening section is tremendous, intensely visual and imaginative enough in style at this stage to justify its mythical pretensions.

The long section on the island is equally resplendent. Alec cuts the stallion loose when the rope around it is wedged in a rock ('You never know when a knife might come in handy', his father has told him, another of his winnings that he has given to the boy as a present). In return, the stallion stamps on a snake that is slithering up to poison Alec's paradise. Gradually the two are drawn together in a bond of mutual trust and daring, the filming rising to the poetry of their relationship by turning their sea games into a kind of underwater ballet. At this juncture, the combination of documentary authenticity with visual awesomeness puts the film on the level of Robert Flaherty's *Louisiana Story*, as well as offering an intriguing variation on the *Robinson Crusoe* myth, with Crusoe as a boy and Man Friday as a black stallion.

What to do, though, when Alec returns home and to the real world? Should one try to sustain the magical, otherworldly atmosphere thus far established, or emphasize the more mundane atmosphere of the second half by way of contrast and comment? Ballard tries to do both and it breaks the film's spine.

Something of the film's visual imagination is certainly sustained. When the stallion has escaped and Alec has failed to find it and falls into a dejected sleep in a doorway, he is awakened by the muffled sound of hoofbeats and a bizarre sight – a carthorse, sporting a Napoleonic hat, emerging out of a blue mist: another quadruped emperor. Alec's test-run on the stallion for the promoters takes place in a ferocious storm, recalling the similar storm that brought boy and horse together; and horse and rider are not seen, the suspense being created through close-ups of stopwatches and the sound of galloping hooves that seem to amplify the mysteriousness of the occasion. After its escape from Alec's back-garden, there is an extraordinary shot of the stallion as it gallops across a dark industrial landscape, almost a Lawrentian symbol of unfettered freedom set across an image of the mechanization of man. At moments like this the spirit of the movie leaps.

Yet there are several things also pulling the film down to earth. The derivative poetic oration at school to welcome Alec home as a hero ('I think that I shall never see/A boy as brave as Alec Ramsey...') is a nice idea in itself but structurally might well be a mistake: the humour dissipates the magical atmosphere too quickly, and it also sets up an expectation of a few ironic games with the stuff of legend that the film fails to deliver. Then there is that huge plot contrivance when, after the stallion's escape, it just happens to end up with a man who is a horse expert and can instantly recognize its pedigree: the movie never quite overcomes that convenient coincidence. The mythological associations of the horse gradually grow much more prosaic and, after being a modern Bucephalus, it is in danger of becoming a four-legged Shane: something mysterious and wild that, even though it acts for the good, cannot entirely be civilized. Moreover, although Mickey Rooney's performance as the trainer is extremely good and worthily nominated for an Oscar, his actual casting is an unfortunate reminder of his role in the thematically similar *National Velvet* (1945), a charming film in its own right but exactly the kind of familiar MGM family fare that *The Black Stallion*, in its opening stages, seemed determined to transcend through its original artistry.

One could argue that the film's second half is meant to stand in stark opposition to the first, to show the confinement of urbanization and adulthood that awaits Alec in contrast to the stallion's natural independence. But this valid concept of a mood of creeping melancholy is belied by

31

the film's ending, when Alec very predictably wins the race. Even Ballard's filming, elsewhere exemplary, comes to pieces here; his complete disbelief in this denouement betrayed by the absence of suspense or surprise and by spatial fakery in the visuals that contrives to make the race look quite nonsensical. In the midst of the frenzied galloping, however, he super-imposes some footage from the island sequence, as if Alec is rediscovering the sense of release he felt in those now far off days. It is a moment that somewhat modifies the empty-headed triumphalism of the race, but it reinforces one's impression of a distinguished, but ultimately disappointing film: namely, that the movie, let alone the hero, should never have left the island.

E.T. – THE EXTRA-TERRESTRIAL
(USA 1982: Steven Spielberg)

Pursued by scientists and adults, a young boy, Elliott (Henry Thomas), is being helped by his schoolfriends to re-unite E.T. with his extra-terrestrial family on their spacecraft. 'Can't he just beam himself up?' asks someone reasonably, to which Elliott replies, in exasperation, 'This is *reality* . . . .'

A joke, of course, from the cinema's most successful blockbusting fantasy for children, but not entirely so. After all Spielberg has suggested that this is his most personal movie, implying by this that it is his most autobiograph-ical: a suburban setting, like his own background, a young hero, like himself, whose father has deserted the family. Then there is the shooting style, which takes some trouble to present a convincing child's-eye-view of the world. Until late in the film most of the adults, like the biology teacher or the leader of the scientific team, who is identified exclusively by his keys, are never seen above waist, i.e. child level. Metaphorically speaking, this also has the effect of bringing adult viewers to their knees, which might explain the hushed reverential tones of some of the reviews. Spielberg also boldly described the film as being about 'the views and values of modern American kids'. He is very good on the behavioural quirks of children: the precise way they feign illness to miss school; the conflict and interaction between different age ranges within a family, as each member strains to gain attention; the glee with which children seize on an opportunity to disrupt the formality of a school lesson; and their inimitable perversity and curiosity, so that when Elliott says, 'Nobody go out there!' it is an invitation for everyone to jump up and have a look. Spielberg's astuteness with this kind of detail – and one remembers the similar concise sensitivity with which he directed the father/son relationship in *Jaws* (1975) – provides the solid foundation from which the fantasy can build, and it is in that sense that *E.T.* can be understood as, on one level, 'reality'. Further, Spielberg recognizes and understands the easy co-existence of reality and unreality in the child's world, so that for the child an imaginary or non-human friend can become quite as real and lovable as any actual existing person.

Yet Spielberg also knows all the moves when it comes to movie know-how, and above all he knows his Disney. *E.T.* first of all resurrects the trusted Disney formula for the successful children's/family film: namely, the use of a broadly realistic setting into which one fantastic element or ingredient is introduced. It then plays with Disney references in its modern

Elliott (Henry Thomas)
watches men with lights
coming for E.T. (1982)

context, updating their relevance and resonance. The pursuit of the extra-terrestrial through the forest is a new twist on the hunt-and-fire scene in the wood that brings *Bambi* to an exciting climax; and the famous shot in *E.T.* of the silhouette of the bicycle across the moon is a direct homage to Disney's *Peter Pan* (1952), when the children look up to the sky and see Pan's ship as a moonlit shadow. As if to reinforce the reference, mother is heard reading *Peter Pan* at one stage to her daughter. Like Disney, Spielberg genuinely loves his characters, which not only brings them to life, but also, in the case of both Snow White and E.T., brings them *back* to life.

Beyond being an updated Disney, however, *E.T.* is also a modernization of the traditional fairy-tale. It uses elements of Babes in the Wood, when E.T. is lost in the forest, and Hop o' my Thumb, when Elliott leaves a trail of M&Ms rather than breadcrumbs to enable the alien to find his way back to safety. To heighten the fearful atmosphere of fairy-tale, the film makes mysterious and evocative use of shadow in its visual texture – it is a strikingly nocturnal film – and the childlike quality of the fable is further enhanced by the way in which the adults are firmly cut down to size and satirized. One wonderful passage of slapstick shows Elliott's mother (Dee Wallace) so wrapped up in her domestic cocoon that she literally cannot see an intoxicated alien wandering around her living room, even when she distractedly flattens him with the refrigerator door as she puts away the

33

groceries. On another occasion, she fails to spot him when he camouflages himself in a toy closet. 'Grown-ups can't see him' is one of the film's refrains, the reason being that they have lost a child's capacity for instinctive imagination. By the time the men from NASA burst into the film, to examine E.T. as a scientific phenomenon, the children's vision seems so much a part of our own that the scientists look more alien than the alien.

'I've been wishing for this since I was ten years old', says the chief scientist (Peter Coyote) about the encounter with E.T. 'The reason so many adults enjoy Steven Spielberg's films', said the great Polish director Andrzej Wajda, 'is that they appeal to what remains of a child in every adult. I love everything childish in these films. But it's only a film-maker of Spielberg's standing and intellectual independence who can carry it off.'[4] There are sentimental elements to be swallowed, which can be done if it is recognized that what is bringing tears to the adult's eyes (in the audience, as in the film) might be subtly different from that which makes the child cry: that is, not the feeling itself so much as the memory of what it was like to feel *that* deeply, that purely. Also Spielberg is careful to ensure that the sentiment has its justification – the serious theme of *E.T.* has to do with healing the pain of a broken family – and, equally importantly, its counterbalancing humour. The Hallowe'en sequence in the film is very funny, particularly as this is E.T.'s first sight of humanity outside Elliott's household, no doubt causing him to wonder exactly who is supposed to be the more strange. The comedy rises to a climax when Elliott goes missing on Hallowe'en evening, and his distraught mother has to report his disappearance to the police. 'How was he dressed when you last saw him?' asks a concerned cop, to which mother replies tearfully, 'As a hunchback. . . .'

CHAPTER TWO

WAR GAMES

Had his brain been damaged by too many war films?

(J. G. BALLARD, *Empire of the Sun*)

We're going to miss this war, and it's all your fault!

(Billy in *Hope and Glory*)

TWO images: a screaming baby in a pram careers down the Odessa Steps; a simple-minded schoolboy on a London bus reaches out to stroke a dog, before he is blown to pieces by a terrorist bomb. The first image is, of course, from Sergei Eisenstein's *Battleship Potemkin* (1925); the second comes from Alfred Hitchcock's *Sabotage* (1936), his film version of Joseph Conrad's *The Secret Agent*. Neither is strictly speaking a war film, but both deploy children in a way that is characteristic of a war film's strategy - that is, by using the fate of children as an amplification of horror. Children do not cause such outrages but they are often caught up in them.

Children are the war film's handiest symbol of innocent victims, and their fate is designed to register on adult sensibilities. Douglas Sirk's *Battle Hymn* (1956) builds a whole picture out of an airman's remorseful response to the knowledge that the German target he obliterated was an orphanage. When a director wishes to elicit an immediate emotional response from a situation of wartime conflict, he often zooms into a close-up of an injured or wailing child, as Roland Joffe does in *The Killing Fields* (1984). The tactic can be self-defeating. Because of television news, we have become more used to such images than formerly and are regrettably a little desensitized. Moreover, we are more accustomed to the visual signs of intrusive television reporting and are more wary of such filming as a conscious emotional effect, verging on the manipulative, as in the Joffe example. A scene in Roger Corman's war movie, *The Secret Invasion* (1964), makes a similar point but more imaginatively and affectingly. A stone-faced Henry Silva puts his hand over

a baby's mouth to stop it crying whilst Nazis are patrolling the area. Only when the danger has been averted and he lifts his hand does he realize he has accidentally suffocated the child. The fact that the death has been caused by the hero, and that the film concentrates on his tears (rather than a child's) at what he has done, contribute to making the point about the innocent victims of war all the more moving.

World War II's most famous child is Anne Frank, whose diary and whose sustained humanity under adversity ('In spite of everything I still believe that people are basically good at heart') became an overwhelming indictment of Nazism. George Stevens's film of her two years in hiding, *The Diary of Anne Frank* (1959), is a powerful document, not only through Stevens's characteristic sensitivity in handling childhood experience, but also because of his personal commitment to the project, borne out of his traumatic experience of being one of the first American film-makers to witness and capture on film the concentration camps at Dachau. Another harrowing fictional example of the suffering of children in wartime occurs in Alan J. Pakula's film version of William Styron's *Sophie's Choice* (1982), a holocaust version of 'Hobson's Choice', where a mother at Auschwitz has to choose between her two children, and gives up her baby daughter. The human spirit is broken by using children as a cynical, sinister bargaining counter. The film's main fault lies in its producing this as its shocking grand climax, rather than implying that this kind of wartime obscenity was being replayed day after day.

If children avoid becoming the victims of war they do so often at a certain cost: their innocence is compromised. In a film like *Empire of the Sun* war destroys a boy's childhood. In Elem Klimov's Soviet war film, *Come and See* (1985), which takes its inspiration from Dostoevsky's maxim that 'a human being is an abyss opening up before you', war pitches children into a premature confrontation with death and with hideous adult cruelty: by the end, an 11-year-old boy looks at least 30. In war films about the behaviour of people under foreign occupation, such as Laile Mikkelsen's *Little Ida* (1981) and Louis Malle's *Au Revoir, les Enfants* (1987), children have to face up to moral choices of a complexity that would have taxed the most sophisticated adult - of loyalty to parents and friends contending with fear, nationalism and struggle for survival. An interesting variation of the 'growing up fast' theme is provided in Volker Schlondorff's film of Günter Grass's novel *The Tin Drum* (1980), the tale of Oskar who refuses to grow up and defiantly marches to the sound of his own drum. Grass's setting of his tale in the Nazi era is double-edged: a grotesque version of *Peter Pan* for a modern age; and a metaphor for Germany's infantilism during this period, when instinctive prejudice raised its head and intelligence went to sleep.

Some films exploit a correlation between war and childhood — both periods of chaos and anarchy, and a loosening of society's rules. War intensifies the life around a child and might even make life seem more exciting. It means fireworks in the sky, fewer days at school, and possibly less disciplining from elders who are now more preoccupied with looking after themselves. There is great dramatic value in the incongruity of the child's reaction to the events of war, because of not being old enough to perceive, understand or respect the 'appropriate' adult response. This

The sadness of wartime evacuation: Geraldine Muir (left) and Sebastian Rice-Edwards (right) in *Hope and Glory* (1987)

incongruity is a comic sub-theme of John Boorman's *Hope and Glory* (1987); it is the serious main theme of René Clement's classic *Jeux Interdits* (Forbidden Games) (1952).

In war films children as symbols of the future have an extra urgency. They represent a hoped-for new generation that will eradicate war and rebuild a new society. This is the meaning and the poignancy of the children's return to the city at the end of Roberto Rossellini's *Rome – Open City* (1945), and of the beautiful fantasy sequence of Joseph Losey's *The Boy with Green Hair* (1948), when the ghosts of war orphans encounter the boy in a glade, give him a perspective on his own problems and see in him a symbol of an optimistic future that has learned from the horrors of the past: 'Green is the colour of spring – it means hope.' 'Are you going to have greed and money and power ousting decency from the world?' asks E. M. Forster's troubled commentary to Humphrey Jennings's *A Diary for Timothy* (1945), as a baby is born into an uncertain post-war environment, soon to be under the cloud of possible global annihilation. Forster poses his question about the future in terms of decency but, for children, the question might have more relevance if posed in terms of adult absurdity. In Bill Douglas's autobiographical *My Childhood* (1972), the only person to show the little boy any comradeship is a German prisoner of war. In John Krish's skilful

Millie Perkins in the starring role in *The Diary of Anne Frank* (1959)

Dean Stockwell as the boy with post-war problems in Joseph Losey's allegorical fantasy, *The Boy With Green Hair* (1947)

Children's Film Foundation production *Friend or Foe* (1983), two English boys find themselves assisting two German soldiers in hiding, partly because their original story about discovering the soldiers had not been believed by their insufferable elders, and partly because one of the soldiers has saved one of them from drowning. Yet should they not be in the business of taking an enemy's life? Everything builds with implacable logic to a conclusion stated by one of the boys in a tone of flat finality: 'I think war's stupid.'

THE SEARCH
(Switzerland/USA 1948 : Fred Zinnemann)

Producer Lazar Wechsler had the idea for *The Search* after coming across a fine book of photographs by Therese Bonney called *Europe's Children*. He thought of Fred Zinnemann as director after seeing Zinnemann's film about Nazism in pre-war Germany, *The Seventh Cross* (1944), and feeling that here was a Hollywood film-maker who really understood the European situation. Also Zinnemann's background in documentary (he had been an assistant to Flaherty in the 1930s, and made his directing debut in the Mexican drama-documentary *The Wave* in 1935) was another undoubted bonus. At the outset, Wechsler, Zinnemann and the writer, Richard Schweizer, agreed that they ought to get as many elements of the story as possible from first-hand observation, visiting the actual locations and talking to as many people as they could. Permission was obtained from the military to go into the occupied zone of Germany and to visit all the United Nations Relief and Rehabilitation Administration (UNNRA) camps. It was here that they first heard the harrowing stories of the concentration camps and began the delicate task of casting the children, explaining to them the purpose of the film and ensuring that the revival of memories of their experience would not be damaging or too painful. Even so, Zinnemann has said that the clothes, or the sight of a uniform, still retained the power to shock. He found it impossible to communicate in German with the Czech boy, Ivan Jandl, who played the main part, even though the lad understood the language. It induced in him a mental block that must have been similar to that described by Sylvia Plath in her semi-autobiographical novel *The Bell-Jar* when recalling traumatic memories of her German-speaking parents: 'Each time I picked up a German dictionary or German book, the very sight of those dense, black, barbed-wire letters made my mind shut like a clam.'[1]

The difficulty was that, after researching the material and being overwhelmed by what they had seen, Wechsler and Zinnemann still did not have a precise focus for the film. Richard Schweizer had not accompanied them on the research because he had pneumonia. When told of the problem, he said: 'Why not make the film around the situation of a mother and son who have been separated during the war?' This dramatic structure enabled them to use their research and flesh out the case histories. The mother (Jarmila Novotna) searches for her son across a devastated Europe, whilst the boy who escaped from an UNNRA truck under the impression he was being taken to a death camp, is discovered by an American soldier, Ralph Stevenson (Montgomery Clift), who unofficially adopts him and prepares to take him back with him to America.

Stylistically, *The Search* is an odd mixture of MGM tear-jerker and documentary authenticity. Its basic situation is potentially sentimental, but it is stiffened by the influence of Italian neo-realism (in its location shooting, its use of little-known actors rather than stars to intensify audience identification, its post-war setting, the urgency and seriousness of its theme and its stress on the experience of children). It comes out of a new realist mood in Hollywood, particularly spearheaded by directors like Frank Capra, William Wyler, John Ford, John Huston and George Stevens who had served in the war and been deeply marked by the experience. Its originality, however, stems from the fact that not only does it underline the horror of the European experience, but also points out the inadequacy in understanding of the American response. The point is inadvertently underlined by the grafting on to the film of a patronizing narration, which was added behind the director's back and which is excruciating enough to have alienated the critic James Agee, who ordinarily would have been expected to be sympathetic: at one point he grumbles, 'while starving children grab for bread, a lady commentator informs one that they are hungry, and that the bread is bread'.[2]

A good example of this limitation of understanding is the scene when the American family of Stevenson's friend, Jerry Fisher (Wendell Corey), arrives at Fisher's flat. The American boy boasts of his family's standard of living: the European boy is painfully rediscovering the quality of life. Around the dinner-table, the wife is rather surprised that the boy looks quite well and can speak English and she behaves towards him as a foreigner to be talked about rather than to be addressed in person. This awkwardness is nicely emphasized in the scene's visual organization, with the child under discussion actually being excluded from the frame for much of the time. Suddenly the American boy has soup accidentally spilt on him and he runs simpering into the arms of his mother. One cannot help comparing the American boy's reaction to a scalded hand and the refugee's tight-lipped stoicism about his horrific experience. Indeed, it has been his refusal to cry out in pain earlier – when the soldiers have applied iodine to his injured foot – that has caused them to wonder who he is and about his former existence. The shot of American mother and son is not to be interpreted as an image of ideal family life endorsed by the film and to which the refugee aspires. It seems rather the shot of a pampered child and matriarch, watched by a boy whose own pain such people can scarcely begin to comprehend. Through the children, it raises the whole question of the role and attitude of Americans in the film.

The American soldier who helps the boy is well-meaning and kindly but limited, as if he does not quite know what he is dealing with. It is to Montgomery Clift's great credit (and one of the reasons why the performance is such a remarkable one) that he understands this so well, refusing to turn the man into an American boy scout and instead offering a sensitive portrayal of a vulnerable and caring man clumsily attempting to come to terms with a situation that he is initially ill-equipped to handle. The American's actions are sometimes clumsy – at one stage he even threatens the boy with a hypodermic needle – but his instincts and intentions are sincere.

The relationship between the two is sensitively done. The American first sees him in the rubble of Munich and tempts him with food, like an animal. It is a reminder of the boy's previous bestial existence, and of the arrival of the children at the UNNRA camp in cattle trucks. The animal imagery is extended as the boy follows the American like a faithful dog and has the concept of mother explained to him through animal pictures, including Bambi (who was also brutally separated from his mother). Such imagery reaches its climax, perhaps, when the boy knocks over Fisher's goldfish bowl, a moment which characterizes both the boy's and the American's state as that of 'fish out of water'. The goldfish gasping for breath recall the boy's near drowning and his death-in-life at the prison camp. Their rescue by the Americans anticipates his fate.

Stevenson initiates a programme in which the lad is to learn English and prides himself on his skill, though the hint is given that the boy had learnt English at home (the mother speaks good English) and is remembering the language rather than being taught from scratch. This education is offered mainly in the form of pictures of New York, of Abraham Lincoln, of Bambi. It is as if he is educating the boy into the ways of America, and his gift to him at the UNNRA camp is to be that most American of symbols, a baseball bat. Yet the visual strategy of the film is precisely to reverse that. If education is a key theme in *The Search*, it is not the education of the European in the ways of America but the education of the American audience to what happened to Europe. Like Stevenson, Zinnemann does it by pictures.

He does it by evoking a family background for the boy that is strikingly different in kind from the life of the American family. The boy's father is a doctor and amateur musician, and family life there is presented in the form of chamber music, with father, mother and daughter playing a trio, and the son writing at a desk. The image is both intensely European and an image of a cultural background that the Nazis are brutally to destroy. This destruction is signalled here by a jarring ring of the doorbell, which cuts atonally across the music's harmony, and by a fade from a shot of some branches visible through a window of their home to a shot of the window of their camp with barbed wire visible.

Similar window shots are to recur in the film, indicative of spurned people trying to re-enter and involve themselves again in the world: like the mother at the chapel, looking through the window for her son whose discovery at that point would alone give her life meaning; like the son later, who has run away from the dinner party into town and looks through the window of a house in search of his mother. Their parting at the prison camp has been shot from behind the wire, the mist across the screen giving the scene a ghostly, nightmarish aura: and such imagery is to gather cumulative force. The boy flinches at the sight of the railings outside the Americans' house because they remind him of prison bars; bridge railings are reflected in the river like bars when the mother thinks of suicide after being told her son is dead; the boy suddenly starts drawing lines across paper as a signal that he is remembering his parting from his mother. Faded Nazi insignia on the UNNRA walls chillingly evoke the hateful memories that can never be entirely erased from the children's minds. Such pictures of a devasted Europe and suffering children are really directed at an American audience in the hope of opening their eyes to a horror they have not all grasped.

'Let's reconstruct a kid's life for a change, instead of building bridges', says Stevenson, who has previously been building a model bridge in the apartment. It is a measure of the film's humanity that the theme of post-war reconstruction is seen not simply in terms of places, but also of people, of psychology. It is also a measure of the film's maturity that it is sympathetic to but not uncritical of a well-meaning America, whose self-image as saviour is modified by images of suffering and by failures of perception. Significantly, the Americans throughout the film are in urgent need of interpreters. They have much to offer, much to learn. For once, it is the innocence of the adults that might be corrupted by confrontation with the horrifying experience of these old, old children.

FORBIDDEN GAMES – JEUX INTERDITS
(France 1952 : René Clément)

France, 1940. A little girl Paulette (Brigitte Fossey), whose parents have been killed during a German bomber attack on a bridge outside Paris, is found wandering forlornly in a wood by a peasant family and temporarily given shelter. One evening she overhears a stray remark about the tragedy on the bridge, to the effect that there were not enough coffins for all the dead and the rest had to be buried 'like dogs'. 'At her age one doesn't realize', says one of the speakers when he suspects Paulette might have been listening.

In fact, all the tensions, misunderstandings, and tragedies that are to come are to stem from this overheard fragment. For her dog has also been killed in the raid and, with the aid of the family's youngest son, Michel (Georges Poujouly), she resolves to bury her dog properly and find a cross for its grave. Finding other dead animals in the countryside, they steal other crosses and establish a pet cemetery in a deserted mill. When Michel's elder brother Georges (Jacques Marin) dies, they steal a wheelbarrow-load of crosses from the village graveyard. Just as their obsession begins to intensify towards morbidity, so does it increase tension amongst the adults, particularly when the family begins to suspect their hated neighbours of desecration.

'It took me five years of patient negotiations to convince the producer', said René Clément when talking about the difficulty of setting up the film. 'Then, although the censors never touched it, certain producers and critics tried to scuttle the film: it was refused by the selection committee for the Cannes Film Festival . . .'[3] Although it is now acknowledged as a classic of world cinema, and in 1979 was voted by the French Academy of Cinema Arts as the eighth best French film ever made, it is still possible to appreciate the discomfort it originally provoked. Its tone is not serious, solemn or sentimental, but sardonic, satirical and strange. There is a strong element of the grotesque not only in the actions of the children, but also in the buffoonery of the peasants ('It's Georges's cross!'/'So it is – it's still got the price on the back'). Indeed, by copying the rituals of adult worship, the children may be exposing its hollowness. Moreover, they may even be usurping the authority of the Church and challenging its monopoly on death.

The subject is childhood but the imagery and language are saturated with

death. 'Cross my heart and hope to die' has never sounded a more sinister childhood pledge. The bizarreness of their obsession is taken to an extreme, since Michel kills a cockroach specifically for their act of devotion, and they become collectors of the materials of death (for example, the altar cross), which they plan to use for purposes of adornment more than symbolism. This seems less consciously sacrilegious than a purely innocent enterprise in copying adult worship, which unfortunately has implications beyond their understanding. Also the morbidity of their obsession probably stems from their premature proximity to death, which makes for a poignant conjunction of elements: a babes-in-the-wood ambience, but with the wood smelling of corpses.

What interested Clément most was the situation of the girl. The opening scene of the aerial bombardment of the bridge, where she loses her parents, could hardly have been more brutally, effectively done: a series of vivid contrasts between animal and human, the mechanical precision of the bombers and the chaos of the panic-stricken people as a car gets stuck, a horse stampedes. In a daze of shock, Paulette has been clinging to her dog.

Babe in the wood: Brigitte Fossey, whose parents have been killed in a bombing raid, meets up with some help in *Forbidden Games* (1952)

'Can't you see he's dead?' says a woman who pulls it from her and throws it in the water. Everything that follows – the girl, like the dog, helplessly swept along by the tide of events – relates to the desolation and disorientation experienced by the girl after her first confrontation with death. After her escapades with Michel she will be signed away to an orphanage by Michel's father, who is betraying a promise to his son that they can keep Paulette if Michel tells them where the crosses are hidden. That lie is the definitive end of Michel's innocence and he will wreck the crosses and throw them in the mill pond. Meanwhile, at the end, on hearing the name 'Michel', Paulette will drift away from her protectors and become lost in the crowd, swallowed up in the chaos and once again cast adrift in her loneliness.

Pauline Kael once called the film 'the greatest war film since *La Grande Illusion* – neither it should be noted, deals with actual warfare.'[4] Its greatness comes from its observations on the kind of human folly and foolishness that can start wars, particularly in a scene where a fight erupts between feuding families during a burial service. In this audaciously incongruous reversal of convention, a graveyard is suddenly turned into a battlefield. It is about incomprehension, irrational familial hatred, and the kind of adult betrayals that leave lasting scars on the development of the young. From casual cruelty towards children, it is a comparatively small leap to crimes against humanity.

IVAN'S CHILDHOOD
(USSR 1962: Andrei Tarkovsky)

In his book *Sculpting in Time*, Tarkovsky discusses those elements of the original story by V. Bogomolov that particularly attracted him to *Ivan's Childhood*. He was not at all interested in the accurate record of army life, but he was intrigued by it as a war story with very little action, a tale that is basically about reconnaisance and about the interval between missions. This, Tarkovsky thought, would give him the opportunity to explore the atmosphere of war in a new way, with its hyper-tense nervous concentration, 'invisible on the surface of events but making itself felt like a rumbling beneath the ground'.[5] At one moment in the film, Captain Kholin (V. Zubkov) invites Lieutenant Galtsev (E. Zharikov) to listen to what he describes as 'the sound of war': what we hear is an eerie, unnatural silence. The main fascination of the material for Tarkovsky was the fate and character of the young boy (Kolya Burlyaev), who was later to play the bell-caster in Tarkovsky's *Andrei Rublev* (1966). Ivan was a boy whose character had been destroyed by war, replacing a natural childhood innocence with a kind of obsessive Dostoevskian demon. Also, Tarkovsky thought, nothing better exemplified the monstrousness of war than Ivan's fate – the absolute inexorability and inevitability of his death.

'Treat the lad with kid gloves, he's touchy', says Kholin when Galtsev is checking, with some incredulity, Ivan's story: that this 12-year-old is actually a secret agent. In these early scenes Ivan seems to dominate and bully the adults, particularly when they are attempting to remove him from the action and send him to the comparative safety of a military academy. 'You're not my father!' he says to one of the officers, who knows that Ivan's parents have been killed and is therefore discomfited; and Ivan's strategies are all a bit like that. When he cries, it is not a moment of weakness: it is a calculation that it might get him what he wants. At another stage, his declaration that 'I'm all alone' is not intended to elicit sympathy but to indicate defiance and independence. Having no ties, he can take more risks.

War has turned Ivan into a vessel of hatred and revenge. Even his children's games are war games. One remarkable sequence shows him as he plays alone in a shelter, with a knife and torch. A beam of light illuminates a message that has been scrawled on the wall, 'Avenge us', and Ivan's game becomes a fantasy enactment of vengeance, in which the stylized sound-track and vivid imagery evoke the horror of war but, more particularly, the distortion of a child's sensibility. In another scene, when looking at Albrecht Dürer's *The Apocalypse*, Ivan insists on interpreting the drawings in the contemporary terms of his own experience and hatred. 'They (i.e. the Germans) haven't changed . . . always trampling on people.' 'It isn't real', says Galtsev to him, to which Ivan snaps back 'Yes, it is, I've seen them'. Nothing it seems – neither game nor art – can ameliorate Ivan's bitterness nor deflect him from his dreadful destiny.

Ivan accompanies Kholin and Galtsev on his final reconnaissance mission behind enemy lines. It is a journey across a dead, flooded forest, just one example of the film's highly charged response to landscape. One thinks also of a love scene between Kholin and the nurse, Masha, in a birch wood and their sudden embrace taking place astride a trench, as if to express the precariousness of emotional ties at times like these and yet the importance of clinging to one's humanity. At another stage a forest of white birches and a wilderness of burnt black stumps are caught in frame together, and it is an image with enormous resonances about Ivan's childhood: his blighted youth, a natural growth overtaken by the blackening of his innocence, a symbol of life and death in precarious balance. During his final journey across the dark water, Ivan will pass the bodies of two compatriots hanging from a tree as a warning against resistance: he is unknowingly witnessing his own approaching death.

The film leaps forward to the end of the war and to a devastated Berlin. Newsreel footage gives evidence of more victimized children, showing the bodies of Goebbels's children, whom he has poisoned before killing himself. Now physically scarred, Lieutenant Galtsev is wandering amidst drifting plaster and fallen leaves in an ex-Gestapo bunker in Berlin and looks down at an officer sifting sadly through the files of people who have been executed by the Gestapo. Suddenly, staring at Galtsev, is a Gestapo photo of Ivan, who has been hanged. Ivan's haunting face is the film's main image and its most poetic landscape: blackened, defiant, with tight nervous lips and dark angry eyes, a face aged by horror, that has seen its own apocalypse.

Described like this, *Ivan's Childhood* might seem simply to be another example of the kind of Soviet film-making – that is, cinema which patriotically developed its war theme through the experience of ordinary people but with virtuoso camerawork – that particularly flourished in the thaw that followed Stalin's death. In other words *Ivan's Childhood* seemed at the time in the tradition of such classics as Mikhail Kalatozov's *The Cranes are Flying* (1957) or Grigori Chukrai's *Ballad of a Soldier* (1960): more intense in effect, but not very different in kind. To some degree this is true, and one could certainly describe *Ivan's Childhood* in the terms in which Khacha-turian described Shostakovich's post-Stalin (arguably anti-Stalinist) 10th Symphony: that is, as an 'optimistic tragedy', the story of a victory achieved at a terrible price. Yet there is one crucial aspect of the film not yet mentioned, which sets it apart from the aforementioned films and indicates and anticipates one of the key features of Tarkovsky's future artistic sensibility: the dream sequences. 'When film is not a document', said Ingmar Bergman, 'it is a dream. That is why Tarkovsky is the greatest of them all. He moves with such naturalness in the room of dreams .... All my life I have hammered on the doors of the rooms in which he moves so naturally ....'

There are four dream sequences in *Ivan's Childhood*. In the first, which begins the film, the camera cranes up a tree, there is a shaft of sunlight and we see Ivan playing in some fields before calling to his mother, 'Mother, there's a cuckoo'. Then Ivan awakens into war, from his hiding in a windmill. In the second dream, which takes place when Ivan has fallen asleep after his interrogation by Galtsev, Ivan is by a well with his mother: they look at a reflection of the moon in the water. After looking at Dürer's picture of war, Ivan falls asleep and dreams of travelling in a cart in the rain with a young girl, who might be his sister: apples spill from the cart, and horses, gleaming with rain, stroll up and start eating the fruit. In the last dream, which is the film's final scene after the revelation of Ivan's death,

On the threshold of dream to escape the waking nightmare: Kolya Burlyaev plays the tormented young hero of *Ivan's Childhood* (1962)

Ivan is seen playing on the beach near the water with the girl and his mother, and in the closing shot, the camera again cranes up the tree.

Tarkovsky was always wary of his imagery being interpreted rather than simply being experienced, so it is probably advisable to describe in fairly general terms the impression created by the dreams. The fact that two of these sequences open and close the film is probably significant, since it means that the whole action is surrounded with the aura of dream. The dreams certainly have an effect on the narrative, consciously interrupting the flow of action, perhaps to allow a more contemplative response. More importantly the dreams serve as an attempt to convey something of the inner life of his hero. In this regard, the dreams modify the socialist realism of *Ivan's Childhood*, just as Luis Buñuel uses dream to modify the neo-realism of *Los Olvidados* (1951). (Indeed, 'modify' might be too weak a word: 'undermine' might be closer to the mark.) The dreams are, appropriately enough, quite mysterious: for example, no explanation is suggested in the film as to the reason why Ivan dreams of his mother but not his father. They are also personal and subjective. The first, for example, is actually Tarkovsky's own earliest childhood recollection when he was four and just beginning to know the world. The final shot of the final dream will be recalled at the very end of Tarkovsky's last film, *The Sacrifice* (1985), which is about the future of mankind after a possible nuclear war, which also ends with a child and a tree, and with a dedication to his son in hope and confidence.

Perhaps the most important and noticeable feature of the dreams is contrast. They show Nature at its most beautiful and fertile, in devastating counterpoint to the blasted landscape, desecrated by man, that is the background for the main action. They also show Ivan as a fresh-faced young boy, which makes the final Gestapo photograph of him burn even more terribly into the memory. 'The most beautiful memories are those of childhood', said Tarkovsky, and the abruptness with which the dreams are interrupted is a measure of the brutality with which Ivan's childhood will be curtailed.

HOPE AND GLORY
(GB 1987: John Boorman)
EMPIRE OF THE SUN
(USA 1987: Steven Spielberg)

It seems inevitable to bracket *Hope and Glory* with *Empire of the Sun*. Both appeared at around the same time and offer the writer's semi-autobiographical child's-eye view of World War II. Coincidentally, both were nominated for a clutch of Hollywood Oscars and both failed to win any. Predictably, the critical concensus expressed a preference for Boorman over Spielberg ('so much more subtly and lightly handled than in Steven Spielberg's overblown and costly epic'[6]); though a strict comparison is perhaps not that useful – they are, after all, dealing with very different theatres of war – to my mind, it would not at all be to Spielberg's disadvantage.

'We're going to miss this war and it's all your fault!' So says young Bill Rohan (Sebastian Rice-Edwards) to his mother (Sarah Miles) in *Hope and*

Jim (Christian Bale) is ecstatic when a B-51 attacks his prison camp in *Empire of the Sun* (1987)

Glory when it seems as if the children are to be evacuated to Australia during the Blitz. However, the mother decides at the station that she cannot part from her children. The rest of the film consists of the young boy's experience of war-torn England in 1942, recollected in adult tranquillity and is essentially an autobiographical memoir by Boorman of his own childhood. In contrast to the usual dour realism of the conventional British war movie, Boorman brings a tone of perky human comedy.

'Thank you, Adolf!' cries a young English boy after a German plane has scored a direct hit on his hated school. For the children, the war is experienced mostly as a refreshing time of freedom from the tyranny of teachers and parents. In fact, the film seems less about war than about growing up, and the key symbolic event is the moment in the cricket game when the boy knocks out his father's middle stump with a googly that Dad has originally taught him to bowl. This kind of eccentric detail is matched by an equal quirkiness in performance (particularly a grandly extrovert display as Billy's grandfather by Ian Bannen) and also in imagery. Some of the visual recollections are so peculiar – the manic careerings of a barrage balloon, the children's recitation in gas masks of their multiplication tables – that they go some way towards explaining Boorman's future baroque imaginings on film.

One of the particular fascinations of *Hope and Glory* as film-autobiography is the insight it gives into Boorman's previous work. For example, one of the most emotional scenes occurs when a house fire melts young Billy's toy soldiers of King Arthur and Merlin: one suddenly remembers the opening in flames of Boorman's film of the Arthurian legend, *Excalibur* (1981). The fire sends the family to the country to live with grandfather at his Thames-side bungalow, and the contrast between the corrupted city and the purer, more primitive country recalls the Boorman of *The Emerald Forest* (1985). In particular, important childhood scenes on the river are not only a reminder of his most famous film, *Deliverance* (1972), but are perhaps a key to the recurrent use in his films of water as a symbol of regeneration. In his introductory essay to the published screenplay of the film, Boorman suggests that both his parents regarded the onset of war as representing 'the possibility of deliverance'.[7]

Yet, in drawing on Boorman's first-hand experience, *Hope and Glory* takes him in a new direction, particularly in his presentation of women. Previously all of his films had been solidly male orientated, even chauvinistic. In *Hope and Glory*, as the young boy is surrounded by women in various stages of matrimony, immaturity or undress, Boorman recollects the way the war has brought out a hitherto untapped reservoir of capability and self-sufficiency in women. In Hollywood such a situation was to produce the misogyny of *film noir*: in Britain, and even more unnervingly, it was, according to Boorman, to lead logically to the ascendancy of Margaret Thatcher.[8] Sarah Miles's performance as the mother won rave reviews, as much perhaps because of the Mrs Miniver-type nobility of the character as for the calibre of her acting. Finer still are the performances of Sammi Davis and Susan Wooldridge as the sexually adventurous daughter and sexually charged neighbour, respectively. These characters seem less sentimentally conceived than the mother, more complex and vital.

It is not difficult to see why the film won such high praise. It is probably the best British film about childhood since the Bill Douglas trilogy (which Boorman much admires). Its blend of memory and mirth, childhood fantasy and sexual awakening, makes it a sort of British *Radio Days*. It taps a vein of nostalgia not only for a certain time in British history, but also for a certain kind of British film-making. It seems to combine the romanticism of 1940s Powell and Pressburger with the good-natured cheek of *Hue and Cry* (1947). A scene where Billy's mother attends a concert recital of Beethoven's *Appassionata* is similar to a moment in Humphrey Jennings's *A Diary for Timothy* which, like Boorman's film, is a celebration of social cohesion and a speculation about the Britain that its children will inherit after the war is over. Indeed, even without the benefit of the later film's perspective, Jennings and his scriptwriter, E. M. Forster, seem much less indulgently nostalgic than Boorman and have a greater sensitivity to a sense of loss, regret and precariousness.

For all its sympathetic qualities, there are several reservations that surface about *Hope and Glory*. It idealizes its characters too much and, as a piece of filming, it seems altogether less adventurous and challenging than Boorman at his best. As often happens with autobiographically inspired pieces, the workings of memory seem to have had an inhibiting rather than liberating effect on the imagination. There is nothing very new or surprising about

Born into an uncertain future: the symbolic new-born child of *A Diary for Timothy* (1945)

Boorman's revelations. Indeed, if one sees the film in conjunction with, say, a reading of David Lodge's excellent novel *Out of the Shelter*, one is aware of a certain familiarity rather than freshness of imagery and situation. As in Boorman, so in the novel: a boy's-eye view of war, the evacuation with the mother to the country, an inadequate father and heroic 'uncle' figure, an elder sister who fraternizes with the allies, the cheerful comic incongruities as children experience a sense of release and adventure, the tentative sexual experimenting, and even the same toys, maps (with the British Empire coloured pink), cricket imagery, and memories of listening for the King's stammer during his Christmas Day broadcasts. The remarkable unanimity of these two memories of war certainly add conviction to its accuracy, but also begin to build up an accretion of cliché and convention. However, whereas Lodge's novel will go far beyond this war background, Boorman's film stays within it, not indulging in the benefit of hindsight, indeed luxuriating in the re-creation.

It is finally the tone that is so offputting. 'How wonderful was the war . . .' says Boorman,[9] and offers this film memoir as the happiest days of his life.

51

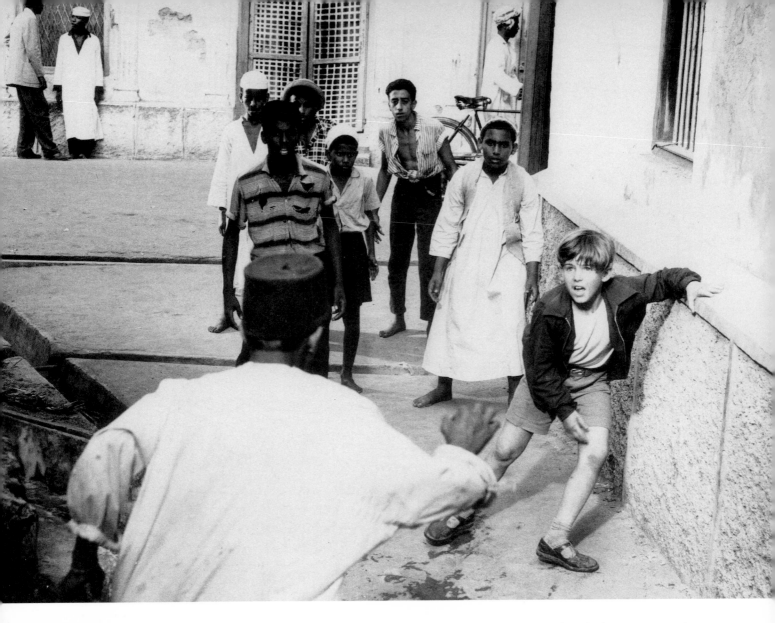

This seems insensitive on at least two levels: to those people who lost loved ones; and to those who regard war as an obscenity that might sometimes be necessary but can never be an occasion for rejoicing. Equally dispiriting is the film's absence of modern perspective. Boorman sympathetically recreates the communal unselfishness and national solidarity of wartime but the relevant response to that mood is not a joyous 'Wasn't it wonderful?' but a sorrowful 'Where did it go?' Boorman's romanticism finally looks less childlike than naïve.

In an interview in the *Independent* newspaper, Steven Spielberg contrasted his film *Empire of the Sun* with *Hope and Glory*, with which it was being widely, and generally unfavourably, compared. 'John Boorman's film is much more positive,' said Spielberg, 'the memories are extremely non-toxic, the boy is going to grow up and lead a normal life, if you can say that of a film director.' By contrast, *Empire of the Sun* is , in the director's words, 'about a very cruel death of innocence'.[10] Based on J. G. Ballard's highly acclaimed novel about his childhood in Shanghai during World War II, it tells the story of a young boy, Jim (Christian Bale), who is separated from his parents in the chaos and confusion that follows the Japanese bombing of Pearl Harbor. The

After being separated from his parents at the outbreak of the Suez crisis, a young boy finds life full of danger in Port Said: Fergus McClelland in *Sammy Going South* (1963)

52

opening of the film seems to owe something to the influence of Alexander Mackendrick's *Sammy Going South* (1962) in its depiction of the separation of child from parents and particularly in the way it gathers to a point of traumatic shock for the boy-hero: the moment when he is vengefully slapped across the face by a person whom he has always regarded as his inferior. It is a slap that signals a brutal division between the old world of comfort and complacency and the new world of scavenging and survival.

Jim will eventually wind up in an internment camp feeling more at home with the raucous, opportunistic Americans, led by Basie (John Malkovich), than with the lethargic, fatalistic British. Spielberg was criticized for presenting the Americans in a more positive light than the British, but he insisted rightly that he was being true to Ballard's novel here. It is a corrective to the myth that the British went through the war with courage, a smile and a stiff upper lip, a myth that *Hope and Glory* endorses. Also it certainly idealizes the Americans much less than Boorman does the British in his film. Contrary to repute, it is a much less sentimental film than Boorman's.

J. G. Ballard has described Christian Bale's performance as Jim as 'the best by a child in the history of the cinema'[11] and, although one can allow for a certain bias on his part, it is by no means a ridiculous claim. Bale has to appear in every scene and has to undergo a complete transformation of character, from the immaculate English schoolboy of the opening scenes to the begrimed and occasionally deranged survivor of later. When he tosses his box of precious childhood possessions into the sea, it is as if his innocence is being carried away in a coffin. His parents do not at first recognize him in the reunion and only in his mother's embrace can he at last close those eyes of his that have seen too much. 'I felt he was yearning for an escape even deeper than his mother's arms', said Spielberg, 'which is why, I think, Ballard in real life turned to science fiction.' It also might explain Spielberg's double identification with his young hero: typically with a child, as so often in Spielberg, particularly in *E.T.* (1982); but also with a child who was to grow up like Spielberg with a fascination for science fiction, as signified particularly by *Close Encounters of the Third Kind* (1977).

Science fiction might seem, in Spielberg's words, a 'deeper escape', but the twist in *Empire of the Sun* is that the boy sees the awesomeness and horror of science's new age. In witnessing from a distance the explosion of the atom bomb ('it was like God taking a photograph'), he sees the future. Part of the fascination of the novel was always its ingenious updating into the nuclear age of the situations of one of the key novels of childhood, Rudyard Kipling's *Kim*. Kipling's hero is very similar to Ballard's, a mercurial personality of constantly shifting identity whose conflicting loyalties lead him to a point of nervous breakdown. Even Spielberg's films, particularly *Indiana Jones and the Temple of Doom* (1984), have had their Kiplingesque qualities. It is not surprising then that the sensibilities of Ballard and Spielberg interlocked so harmoniously on this film. Just as Jim has to learn a new language in his endeavour to endure ('I learnt a new word today – atom bomb'), so Spielberg has made his most adult film about the world of childhood. If Boorman's film represents a temporary regression, Spielberg's looks like a new maturity.

CHAPTER THREE

LITTLE HORRORS

---

*Since that time, which is far enough away
now, I have often thought that few people
know what secrecy there is in the young,
under terror. No matter how unreasonable
the terror, so that it be terror.*

(Charles Dickens, *Great Expectations*)

It's a hard world for little things.

(Lillian Gish in *The Night of the Hunter*)

THE enduring popularity of Grimms' grim fairy-tales has always testified to
a certain relish for the gruesome amongst children and, when tackled about
the morality of making films designed to scare people, Alfred Hitchcock was
fond of pointing out that nearly every child's first pleasurable memory is the
time when he or she was startled by the word 'Boo!' Most children seem to
enjoy the shiver of a good ghost story in much the same way as they scream
with pleasure on a roller-coaster, but a lot inevitably depends on the quality
of the story-teller. As Henry James insisted in his preface to *The Turn of the
Screw* horror is all the more effective when atmospherically evoked in the
mind of the reader or audience rather than graphically spelt out or
demonstrated. Making the same point in an article on horror in the movies,
Tom Milne quotes from Shelley's poem on the 'tempestuous loveliness of
terror', 'On the Medusa in a Florentine Gallery': '. . . it is less the horror than
the grace/Which turns the gazer's spirit into stone.'[1]

Building on the principles of suggestion rather than sensation as
advocated by James and Shelley, films like *Curse of the Cat People* (1944), *The
Night of the Hunter* (1955) and *The Innocents* (1961) have woven poetic webs
of terror around the apprehensive state of childhood. So too does Victor
Erice's highly praised Spanish film, *The Spirit of the Beehive* (1973), which

Caged youth: Linda Manz
as a brutalized teenager
in Dennis Hopper's *Out
of the Blue* (1980)

explores the impact of a showing of *Frankenstein* on a number of small children. Their absence of adult prejudice makes them more fascinated than fearful, and it is a tone that admirably echoes that of the scene in the original between the monster and the little girl, who senses the sensitive soul behind his frightening exterior. The little girl in *To Kill a Mockingbird* will come to a similar realization when the man the children have always feared, 'Boo' Radley, will turn out to be their friend and saviour. As Dickens noted, much of childhood is spent in a state of fear and two of the most powerful representations of childhood terror are in David Lean's masterful Dickens adaptations: the opening scene in the graveyard in *Great Expectations* (1946), when the boy Pip is grabbed by the convict Magwitch, who seems to come at him out of nowhere; and the scene in *Oliver Twist* (1948) when Oliver has to sleep in the room where the undertaker to whom he has been apprenticed keeps the coffins.

In some horror films, by way of contrast, the child is actually the source of

the horror. Writing in 1936 about *These Three* (1936), William Wyler's first film version of Lillian Hellman's *The Children's Hour* (he was to remake it in 1961 with the lesbian theme made explicit), Graham Greene said: 'Never before has childhood been represented so convincingly on the screen, with an authenticity guaranteed by one's own memories. The more than human evil of the lying, sadistic child is suggested with quite shocking mastery by Bonita Granville . . . it has enough truth and intensity to stand for the whole of the dark side of childhood, in which the ignorance and weakness of the many allows complete mastery to the few.'[2] Although in most respects Wyler's 1961 remake is preferable to this version, the girl in the remake does not come near to suggesting the alarming, diabolical intelligence of Bonita Granville in the role – a well nigh definitive performance of the child horror. (When she grew up, she was to become a close political confidante of Ronald Reagan.)

Such a film with such a performance challenges the notion of innocence

Dickensian childhood: the gruesome bedroom of Oliver Twist (John Howard Davies) in David Lean's 1948 film

Centre of attention: the evil child (Bonita Granville) of William Wyler's *These Three* (1936). From left to right: Alma Kruger, Merle Oberon, Miriam Hopkins and Joel McCrae

and is an attack on the Romantic idealization of the child. It seems more an endorsement of the doctrine of original sin, as does a novel like William Golding's *Lord of the Flies*, filmed by Peter Brook in 1963, where a group of public schoolboys degenerate into savagery on a desert island, an experience that leaves its young hero weeping 'for the end of innocence and the darkness of men's hearts'. The fascination with 'wicked' children, though, often comes across as a delight in the anarchic rather than obedient side of childhood. This is something that Joe Dante's horror comic *Gremlins* (1984) exuberantly exploits, for the gremlins are basically recalcitrant brats, and Dante couples this with a comment on the failure of America to bring up its children, largely because the adults are little more than kids themselves. The point is wonderfully driven home in the heroine's mock-horror story of the death of her father, who has suffocated in a chimney on Christmas Eve: 'That's how I discovered there was no Santa Claus.'

Some other films play on the fear felt by children as the social group that is least able to defend itself. The resourcefulness yet vulnerability of the two young boys in Jack Clayton's eerie film version of Ray Bradbury's *Something Wicked This Way Comes* (1983) is a good example of that: they can elude Mr Dark for a while but, to defeat him, they will need help from an adult agency, notably the ageing father of one of the boys. What is particularly interesting in horror films in which children play an important role is the working out of adult/child, and often more specifically parent/child, relationships in a nightmarish form that brings forth precariously suppressed demons. They dramatize in grotesque forms a child's fear of the adult world, and sometimes indeed of his or her parents, who can become overwhelming ogres. The horrors committed by the leading characters in Michael Powell's *Peeping Tom* (1960) and Peter Sasdy's *Hands of the Ripper* (1971) basically stem from their victimization as children by their fearsome fathers, and similarly traumatized is Linda Manz's young heroine in Dennis Hopper's *Out of the Blue* (1982), whose freaked-out father has turned their home into Heartbreak Hotel.

Conversely there are horror films that could be interpreted as projecting an adult fear or even hatred of children as the destroyers of bourgeois marriage, as in *The Omen* (1976), or as perennial reminders of adult guilt, corruption and insufficiency, as in *A Nightmare on Elm Street* (1985). Certainly horror films in the 1970s and 1980s, in their attitudes to children, seem to have veered between twin extremes of protectiveness and paedophobia. As examples of the former, Steven Spielberg's *Something Evil* (1971) and James Cameron's *Aliens* (1986) are Gothic extravaganzas on the unlikely theme of maternal instincts. Conversely *The Exorcist* (1973) and the *Nightmare on Elm Street* series of films have been held up as unsavoury examples of the cinema of sadism, with the victims being children. What do such films tell us about the cinema and, in their popularity, about our society? It is proper for adults to express concern, but equally proper to remember that what we are talking about is not reality but a form of fantasy. Children themselves certainly appreciate the distinction. When the heroine (Sigourney Weaver) is trying to allay the fears of the young girl in *Aliens* by pointing out that her doll is not frightened, the girl is unimpressed. 'It's a bit of plastic', she says.

THE CURSE OF THE CAT PEOPLE
(USA 1944 : Gunther Von Fritsch, Robert Wise)

Although ostensibly a sequel to the highly successful Val Lewton production *Cat People* (1942), and therefore an anticipated horror fantasy, *The Curse of the Cat People* is actually a study of the inner life of a young girl whose loneliness supplies her with an imaginary friend. As is often the case with Lewton's films, its inspiration is not filmic, but literary, in this instance the Robert Louis Stevenson poem 'The Unseen Playmate', which is quoted explicitly in the film:

> *When children are playing alone on the green*
> *in comes the playmate that never was seen.*
> *When children are happy and lonely and good*
> *The Friend of the Children comes out of the wood.*

Prior to the arrival of this 'playmate' the character of the young girl Amy (Ann Carter), is delicately conveyed. She is a dreamer who, according to her worried father Oliver Reed (Kent Smith), has too many fantasies and too few friends. He interprets her solitariness and sensitivity as sulkiness and strangeness but, in his anxiety for her to be assimilated into a group, fails to recognize defects in his own understanding. When no one comes to Amy's birthday party because she has posted the invitations in the hollow of a tree, her father has to explain that when he said it was 'a magic mail-box' he was telling a story, not the literal truth. Yet only a few minutes later at her party, Amy is told that if she blows out all the candles on her birthday cake, 'your wishes will come true'. The girl notices the contradiction but determines to be 'just how Daddy wants me to be'.

Because of the birthday disaster over the invitations however, the children are further alienated from Amy. The tension increases when she visits the old house that the other children describe as 'haunted' and as inhabited by 'witches'. It is, in fact, inhabited by an elderly ex-actress, Julia

Amy (Ann Carter, right) meets the mysterious old lady (Julia Dean) in *The Curse of the Cat People*

Farren (Julia Dean) who takes to Amy and gives her 'a ring to wish on', much to the resentment of the actress's companion, Barbara (Elizabeth Russell), whom she refuses to recognize as her daughter. This encounter leads Amy to another argument with her father, who is building her a model ship to play with but is clearly getting more pleasure out of it than Amy is ever likely to. He does not believe her story about the ring – 'But it's true'/'Let *me* be the judge of that'. At this juncture it is Amy's wish on the ring for a friend that brings forth the spectre of Irena (Simone Simon), who is actually the ghost of Reed's first wife. 'Out of your loneliness', says Irena, 'you called me and brought me into being.'

The father's exasperation at his daughter and his inability to see what she sees will eventually cause her to run away from home. She runs towards the Farren house, where Barbara's jealousy of Amy is turning to murderous hatred. One of the cleverest aspects of the film is the way in which it gradually suggests certain key connections between these two contrasting

Three children spy on a spooky house in *To Kill a Mockingbird* (1962): John Megna (left), Mary Badham (centre) and Philip Alford (right)

60

households. The Farren house is supposedly 'haunted' but, in fact, it is the Reed house that is the more haunted, since the father's disastrous first marriage is one of the key reasons for his excessive anxiety over Amy. Mrs Farren pointedly refuses to 'know' Barbara as her daughter, but on a less literal level, the Reeds seem similarly unable properly to 'know' their daughter. It takes Amy (in a magical moment where she imagines Barbara to be Irena and consequently her friend) to exorcise the ghosts from the two households. Intensity of imagination succeeds where rationality has failed.

For a B-picture, it is interesting how *The Curse of the Cat People* seems to have anticipated the imagery of more prestigious pictures about childhood. The hollow of a tree trunk as a mail-box of mystery, a benevolent haunted house, a girl's point of view – all these foretell the atmosphere of Robert Mulligan's superb film of Harper Lee's *To Kill a Mockingbird* (1962). As in *The Innocents* (1961), a portrait of a dead person comes to life in an active imagination. In Disney's version of *Peter Pan* (1952), a father's final concurrence that he too can see his daughter's vision seems to put him in touch again with the springs of childhood imagination. Still, when Irena appears before Amy to wave goodbye and Amy's father says that he sees her, it is noticeable that he is looking towards Amy rather than towards her vision: it could imply complete trust or, then again, it could suggest he is simply patronizing her. Sometimes the unevenness of execution and performance makes the film more ambiguous than was probably intended.

Nevertheless, all the scenes involving the girl are realized with great sensitivity and skill. The blandness of the Sleepy Hollow home setting is tellingly contrasted with the intensity of Amy's inner life – full of phantoms, fairy-tales, headless horsemen – implying that her imaginary world might in some way be a reaction against the dully rational, conformist and authoritarian world of her parents. Also it explores most delicately that fine line in childhood between 'acceptable fantasy' and 'untruth' and the way parents can sometimes inadvertently impose too much of their own knowledge and sense of fantasy on their child. As in many dream-like stories of childhood (for example, Raymond Briggs's *The Snowman*), the trick is to come up with an ending that both releases the child from the fantasy but at the same time validates it. In *The Curse of the Cat People* Irena is seen by Amy (and by us) but is plainly bidding goodbye. The reconciliation between father and daughter has made the existence of an 'unseen playmate' no longer necessary.

THE NIGHT OF THE HUNTER
(USA 1955 : Charles Laughton)

'It's a hard world for little things', says Widow Cooper (Lillian Gish), as she hears the cry of a rabbit attacked by an owl and resumes her vigil by the children who are preparing to be pounced on by psychopathic preacher Powell (Robert Mitchum). Childhood is often a fearful time, and all its most menacing manifestations – fear of the dark, of ghosts, strangers, adults, loss of one parent, the acquisition of another – are present in *The Night of the Hunter*, perhaps the cinema's most poetic and relentless evocation of childhood terror. Two children, John (Billy Chapin) and Pearl (Sally Jane Bruce), are entrusted by their father (Peter Graves) never to reveal the hiding place of the money he has stolen. It is money for which he has killed and a killing for which he will hang. They are hounded by the Reverend Powell, a psychopathic killer of widows who has shared a cell with their father and who has come to find the money. Powell represents both the threat of the stepfather supplanting their father and a physical and sexual threat, as first the lover and then the murderer of their mother. They must escape, and do so into the arms of Widow Cooper and her brood of children, who will defend them when Powell comes hunting.

The film's style is powerfully primitive, its Expressionist imagery (particularly in the murder scene) recalling *The Cabinet of Dr Caligari* (1919) and old-fashioned devices such as the use of iris shots recalling the style of the silent era. By conjuring up stylistic recollections of cinema in its infancy, Charles Laughton is seeking to approximate visually the instinctive and innocent point of view of the children. (François Truffaut would deploy similar methods for similar reasons in *L'Enfant Sauvage*). According to his brilliant cameraman, Stanley Cortez, Laughton prepared for his directing debut by re-viewing many of the classics of D. W. Griffith. This might account for his casting of Griffith's favourite actress Lillian Gish in a key role. She evokes not only the silent era of Griffith, but also the theme of suffering childhood through memories of her magnificent performance in

Public humiliation for the schoolgirl Jane Eyre (Peggy Ann Garner) in Robert Stevenson's 1944 film. Henry Daniell is the frowning Mr Brocklehurst

Griffith's *Broken Blossoms* (1919) as a child-woman terrorized by her brutal father. The famous scene where she hides in terror in a closet away from her violent father might well have inspired that equally terrifying scene in *Night of the Hunter* where the children hide from Powell in the coal cellar.

The other important aspect of the film's style is its quality of heightened nightmare – childhood as a bad dream from which the child finally awakes, and endures. 'Dream, little one, dream . . .' are the first words we hear. Powell and Widow Cooper seem less like psychological creations than nightmarish configurations: ogre and fairy godmother, respectively. In Robert Mitchum's brilliant black comedy performance, Powell barks and howls like an animal, a cartoon-like figure (like, say, Ted Hughes's Crow) who is nevertheless capable of generating enormous menace. In Lillian Gish's equally expert performance, Widow Cooper resembles the old woman who lives in a shoe. It is a tale that conjures up other tales that have always haunted children's imaginations, from the Big Bad Wolf through Huckleberry Finn (the escape on the river) to Moses and King Herod. But these tales keep turning back into the main one. 'Once upon a time there was a rich King', says John to Pearl, preparing to make them and his father the heroes of his own fairy-tale: instead, it suddenly brings forth the spectre of the prowling Powell – a huge black shadow on the wall. Children's tales and games in the film have a way of rubbing against the horror of the main action, rather than providing any release from it. The children's game of hide-and-seek that opens the film leads to the discovery of Powell's first murder victim. 'Hing-hang-hong, see what the hangman's done', chant the children to John and Pearl after their father's death.

Although it has an element of dream and fairy-tale, the film refers pointedly to the period in which it is set, the 1930s. The lynch-mob out to avenge themselves on Powell have the fervour of a revivalist rally (small matter that their leaders were formerly Powell's most ardent admirers) and bring to mind the harsh portraiture of lynch-mob morality in 1930s classics like Fritz Lang's *Fury* (1936) and Mervyn LeRoy's *They Won't Forget* (1937). Also it shows how the Depression can drive people to crime. In *Night of the Hunter*, as well as being threatened with murder, the children are a motive for it, since the father kills out of horror at seeing children 'roaming the woodland for food . . .'. Later this is exactly what will happen to John and Pearl, and a charity lady whom they encounter will lament 'such times when young'uns roam the road'.

Although rightly celebrated as a film that captures the secret, frightening and yet magical world of childhood, *Night of the Hunter* could be criticized for its element of boy chauvinism: that is, its rather unbalanced treatment of the relationship and contrast between John and Pearl. It is John who is favoured by the father with the secret (the money's hiding place) and entrusted with the responsibility for Pearl. 'It's too much!' John will finally cry, when the arrest of Powell will produce in him the same reaction he had to his father's arrest (clutching his stomach as if stabbed and moaning 'No, no'). He throws the money away and refuses to name or look at Powell during the trial: whether out of fear, trauma, or a recognition of Powell's fateful kinship with his father, it is hard to say. It might well simply be a refusal to look at the face of adult greed and corruption before he is ready:

63

LITTLE HORRORS

his father made the mistake of entrusting him with a burden that was 'too much' for a child. The complexity of John's character and situation is rendered much more completely than that of Pearl. She is presented as dim-witted and shown, in contrast to John's wary resourcefulness, to be completely taken in by Powell, even after he has called her a 'poor, silly, disgusting little wretch' (Mitchum at his wittiest and most withering). Neil Jordan's *The Company of Wolves* (1984), a film which owes a great deal to *Night of the Hunter* for its imagery, nevertheless attempts to redress this balance by making its horror story of Big Bad Wolves for, and about, teenage girls rather than boys.

THE INNOCENTS

(GB 1961 : Jack Clayton)

I seemed to be floating not into clearness but into a darker obscurity, and within a minute there had come to me out of my very pity the appalling alarm of his being perhaps innocent. It was for the instant confounding and bottomless, for if he were innocent, what then on earth was I?

(HENRY JAMES, *The Turn of the Screw*)

Henry James's little pot-boiler of a ghost story, in which a governess tries to exorcise evil spirits from the souls of two children who are, according to her, possessed, has always been one of his most discussed and elusive works. Jack Clayton's eerie and elegant film does full justice to its spine-chilling ambiguity. The film begins in a garden at dead of night, as an anguished governess sobs and whispers, 'I wanted to save the children, not destroy them, I love children more than anything . . .'. As the flashback develops, we have to assess whether this love manifests itself as salvation and sacrifice or suffocation and self-obsession. Have the children really been possessed by demons or are the ghosts the governess sees the product of her neurotic imagination?

Part of the evidence for our assessment comes, of course, from the way the children are characterized, and here again the film catches an essentially Jamesian ambiguity. Children are invariably strange in James, seeming either too beautiful to live or having an innocence that tempts violation. Like other Jamesian children (for example, the young girls in *The Portrait of a Lady* and *What Maisie Knew*), Miles and Flora in *The Turn of the Screw* seem unnaturally precocious, but it is arguable whether this is due to their innate characters or simply an inevitable consequence of the corrupt situations into which their elders have prematurely thrust them.

In the film, Flora (Pamela Franklin) certainly looks 'angelic', but the presence of something more sinister is suggested in a number of tiny details, such as the way she stands at the end of the sleeping governess's bed like an incubus, or her accurate presentiment that her brother Miles is coming when he is not due home from school for some weeks. There is also a streak of cruelty about her attitude to Nature: almost drowning her pet tortoise,

The governess (Deborah Kerr) confronts Flora (Pamela Franklin) with her terrifying suspicions in *The Innocents* (1961)

64

Rupert; watching in fascination as a spider ensnares a butterfly. But does this necessarily add up to evil possession? Her language degenerates as she is driven to the point of near breakdown ('To hear such filth from a child's mouth!') but this might be her only means of protesting against a governess whom she thinks is now completely mad.

Equally disturbing is Miles, played with preternatural poise by the admirable Martin Stephens: he also played the leader of the weird super-intelligent children of *Village of the Damned* (1961), who also have to be destroyed by the adults principally because they terrify them so. Miles is a strange looking boy, a little adult who has the capacity to be a 'deceitful flatterer'. He is sensitive to the absence of parents or relatives who do not have time for their children. Like Flora too, he seems blessed with second sight and magical powers that nevertheless could also have a rational explanation. He can tell when the governess is outside his room and when she exhorts him to 'trust me', his eyes flash and, as if at his bidding, the wind gushes and the candle blows out. At times he does frighten the governess, whether he is jumping on her in a game of hide-and-seek, or offering a recitation that seems to invite ghostly visitation ('Enter my lord/Come from your prison/Come from your grave/The moon has arisen'). But all this might be part of a deliberately naughty ploy, worked out with Flora, to disconcert a governess who is becoming a little too cloying and clinging. When he walks in the garden late at night the governess thinks he is communing with the devil, Quint, but maybe Miles's explanation is equally plausible: he wants her to 'think me bad for a change' and puncture her excessive idealization. Perhaps the passionate kiss he plants on her lips has a similar implication: not evidence of adult possession but, paradoxically, a child's strategy to get the governess to keep her distance in future.

The children might well have been privy to the passionate affair between the valet Quint and the former governess, Miss Jessel, which so alarms the present governess. In this respect, then, it is quite possible that in his sleep Miles might have said things that disturbed his schoolfriends – though, in these circumstances, should not the Head have discussed this with Miles instead of peremptorily expelling him? Nevertheless, in the finale in greenhouse and garden, where governess and Miles confront each other in a hothouse of rage and repression, it is still open to interpretation whether Miles is really possessed by Quint or whirling in total bewilderment at the governess's hysteria. 'Say his name!' she insists. 'Who?' he asks. Finally he gets her drift and shouts Quint's name, but when he says, 'There – you devil', he is looking at the governess, as if it is her face that truly terrifies him. The last word on his lips, before he collapses and dies of heart failure, is, 'Where?' In an exact reversal of *The Curse of the Cat People*, it might be the adults who are seeing visions and the children who exasperatedly dispute them.

Deborah Kerr is particularly marvellous in this last scene. 'I have you . . .' she says to Miles, as if she is now the spirit of possession. On realizing he is dead she cries his name and her head flops back in horror, like that of the dead pigeon she has found under his pillow. Only then, alone with the dead body, can she kiss Miles, deliberately and with intent, full on the lips. 'She was in love', said the narrator in James's story, adding yet another layer of ambiguity: did he mean with the uncle, or with Miles? 'Give me your hand, give me your promise ...' the uncle (Michael Redgrave) has said to the governess in the film. He means her pledge to look after the children, but it comes out sounding like a proposal. 'O, Miss, are you afraid he'll corrupt you?' laughs the housekeeper Mrs Grose (Megs Jenkins) when the governess is musing over Miles's expulsion. 'Wait 'til you see Miles again before you judge me', says the governess to Mrs Grose. She is never to see Miles again. What, then, is our judgement of the governess?

The children are not 'innocent' – that is, they are precocious, play wicked games – but maybe it is not they whose innocence has been corrupted, but the governess whose innocence is corrupt. Evil in *The Innocents* does not come in the form of sexual demons but in a set of attitudes that sees sexual knowledge as evil, the villains therefore being Miles's unseen headmaster who has outragedly expelled him without explanation, and a governess driven to the point of hysteria by her horror of sexuality. In Clayton's film – and it seems a perfectly valid reading of James's 'lurid, poisonous little tale' (Oscar Wilde) – the monsters are not Quint and Jessel but the values and repressions of Victorianism.

THE NANNY

(GB 1965: Seth Holt)

There is an interesting moment in *The Nanny* when the young boy, Joey (William Dix), is talking about the nanny whom he hates to his friend next door, Bobby (Pamela Franklin). 'She stuck up for you, didn't she?' says Bobby. 'Who?' says Joey. 'Mary Poppins', she replies.

On one level, this in an in-joke. Improbable as it may now sound, Bette Davis, who plays the role of Nanny in this film, was once seriously considered for the role of Mary Poppins in the Disney movie. On another level, the remark abounds in irony. Joey's parents treat Nanny as if she actually were Mary Poppins – a devoted domestic who marvellously lightens the family load – and are deaf to Joey's protestation that this Mary Poppins is trying to kill him.

Gradually the tragedy at the heart of the film is revealed. Joey's young sister has drowned in her bath. Joey has been blamed but he has insisted that Nanny was responsible. Adult society has inevitably sided with Nanny's version of events, and the boy has been incarcerated in a psychiatric hospital. When he is due to come out, his mother (Wendy Craig) is too frightened even to go and meet him and Nanny must accompany his father (James Villiers) on the journey. In a meeting between the father and the head of the institution, Dr Beamaster (Maurice Denham), the doctor makes a distinction, rather like that in *Curse of the Cat People*, between 'mental fantasies that are normal and those that are abnormal'. Joey does indeed seem a little odd, pretending before he goes to have hanged himself in front of the hospital matron.

Because Nanny is so good and the boy seems so bad, there is no real surprise when the balance begins to reverse: if it did not, there would be no film. On the other hand, the film gets round this seeming predictability by a number of judicious devices: a complex structure that keeps returning to the tragedy from several different angles, and a complicated psychology in

which the action of the boy and Nanny are open to a variety of interpretations and explanations. For example, the boy's fake hanging might seem an indication of his 'badness' ('an unkind joke', says the liberal doctor), yet its significance is not the joke itself but on whom it is being played: a 'Nanny' figure in the institution. Then there is Joey's home, which is basically run by Nanny in the face of an indifferent father and a weak and immature mother. (Mother has tormented herself earlier by remembering her little girl's plaintive comment, 'When I grow up, when I grow up . . .', but the line seems as much applicable to her as to her child.) Joey has no privacy – there is no key in the bathroom and he forces Nanny to swear that she will not come in – and he is not trusted or believed. His hatred of Nanny, then, is not simply physical fear but her disproportionate influence in the family, which prevents him establishing any relationship with his parents. It is this frustration that causes him to say that he hates his mother and, when his father is going away: 'I hope you don't come back'.

Nanny (Bette Davis) exudes charm but the boy remains unimpressed: after all, his meal might be poisoned. William Dix as the boy; James Villiers as his father in *The Nanny*, (1965)

68

A nurse has described Joey as 'a monster' but gradually it is revealed that Joey has been telling the truth and that Nanny did indeed cause his sister's death. Yet Nanny is not a monster either for it was entirely an accident, caused when she routinely switched on the bathwater tap and walked away preoccupied without noticing that, behind the curtain, the girl had fallen in the bath and knocked herself unconscious. The horror around the bath has obvious echoes of Hitchcock's *Psycho* (1960), as does the film's device of monologues to the dead. However, as the film returns obsessively to this accident, showing it from different points of view, as well as showing two replays and variations of the accident (a trick version, and the real one), the whole incident becomes more intricate, more tragic. Seth Holt's editing experience tells here: all the complex implications of what has happened are marvellously assembled.

It seems that what has happened is that Nanny, on this fateful afternoon, has just come from her own daughter's deathbed, a daughter she has neglected because of her commitment to service and who is dying because of a botched abortion. The accident with the little girl has quite credibly driven Nanny into a desperate act of self-protection by unloading her guilt onto someone else. Admitting her culpability would undermine the structure of her entire existence, making her life-long neglect of her daughter in favour of her alternative family quite pointless.

The film works out its denouement with considerable skill and finesse. Joey's aunt, Penelope (Jill Bennett), has begun to suspect Nanny's threat to Joey when she sees her near the boy's door with a pillow. Nanny says she felt he might need one, but Penelope recollects from her childhood that Nanny does not approve of pillows for children. Unfortunately for Penelope, the shock precipitates a heart attack and, in a neat homage to one of Bette Davis's most famous screen moments from Wyler's *The Little Foxes* (1941), Nanny refuses to move and get her medicine. Joey is now at her mercy and in his desperate desire to escape he, like his sister, slips and knocks himself unconscious. However, in the act of submerging the unconscious boy in the bath, her nanny instincts re-emerge: she pulls him out, and the truth emerges. Far from seeming a weak conclusion, the cross-cutting between her attempted murder and the original accident is so brilliant and Bette Davis's performance so moving, that her final 'rescue' of Joey seems almost like a resurrection of the little girl and, for the nanny, an act of fantasy fulfilment in which she is given a chance to redeem herself and reverse the original tragedy.

The Nanny is a remarkably restrained and compelling Hammer horror film. It has less in common with Hammer's usual horror rhapsodies than with, say, Joseph Losey's *The Servant* (1963), matching the Losey film in the subtlety with which it photographs the house (at times making it look like a doll's house, at other times a fortress, and at others more like an embassy than a home). But if there is one British film it recalls above all others, it would be Alexander Mackendrick's *The Ladykillers* (1955), that savage black comedy about a nanny-ridden Britain. Holt, who was associate producer on that film, has rendered its Ealing theme in terms of Hammer horror.

It seemed a quaint theme in the egalitarian, youth-dominated Swinging

69

Sixties era in which *The Nanny* first appeared but, post-Thatcher, it looks remarkably prophetic, and indeed a political allegory. The film's wet upper-class parents think Nanny is marvellous and take no notice of the young boy in the household who keeps screaming that Nanny's medicine, which she insists is necessary, is actually poisoned. Make what you will of the fact that he is eventually proved right and that Nanny, whilst professing concern, is shown to be completely off her rocker. By then, it is almost too late.

THE EXORCIST
(USA 1973: William Friedkin)

As everyone must know by now, *The Exorcist* is the story of a 12-year-old girl, Regan (Linda Blair), who is possessed by the Devil. This possession takes the form of a drastic deterioration of civilized behaviour. Regan mouths obscenities, urinates on the carpet, spews over a local priest, and precipitates someone else's suicide. No precise reason is given for this particular girl's possession other than her interest in the supernatural; and no special reason is given for the form it takes or for the victims it singles out for punishment, other than being a tenuous extension of Regan's disapproval of her mother's life-style (her swearing, her divorced status, her emancipation). It is possible to see the child as a punishment for the 'transgressions' of her mother. In that sense, *The Exorcist* might be seen as a logical extension of the Gothic Puritanism of Nathaniel Hawthorne's nineteenth-century classic *The Scarlet Letter* taken to a modern extreme, with Regan the equivalent of Pearl and her mother the equivalent of Hester (her badge of shame being 'A for Actress; or A for Agnostic').

Like *Carrie* (1975) and *The Shining* (1980), *The Exorcist* probes the uncanny in ostensibly 'normal' children. Like *The Bad Seed* (1956), *The Innocents*, *The Children's Hour*, *Lolita* (1961) or the British TV movie *Poison Candy* (1988), it is a continuation of the tradition of 'sinister' little girls. In *The Exorcist*, Regan is a force of pure destruction, desecrating religious symbols, defiling her spotless home, defying figures of authority. Her name might be significant, an evocation of one of the demonic daughters of King Lear who brings chaos.

The Devil invades the child's body on the verge of adult sexuality, and it also invades her voice (the part being voiced here by Mercedes McCambridge). It is not simply the theme of evil that disturbs but its graphic depiction, all the more uncomfortable because the girl seems simultaneously the agent of evil and also its helpless victim.

Although ultimately the film is about the triumph of Good, Faith and Family and might even be seen as an apologia for the Catholic Church – a sort of Gothic *Going My Way* – for many the film leaves a nasty taste in the mouth. Who is the film for? It is aimed at an adult audience, which is invited to be entertained or gripped by the visual spectacle of a child's suffering. 'As a father', said John Boorman prior to the making of the film's very different sequel, *Exorcist II – The Heretic* (1977), 'I found the book extremely tasteless, cruel and sadistic towards children.'[3] It was a view shared by Max Von Sydow, who plays the exorcist in the film and who was rather horrified by the final product whose popularity, he thought, played on an audience's latent hatred of children. According to Boorman, Von Sydow believed that

Exorcizing the devil:
Linda Blair (left), Max
Von Sydow (centre) and
Jason Miller (right) in *The
Exorcist* (1973)

the root of this hatred was an unconscious fear of overpopulation and a consequent feeling that children nowadays pose a threat more than signify a blessing: for that reason, audiences were encouraged to enjoy watching a child tortured on screen. The critic R. S. Prawer felt a similar discomfort with Richard Donner's Antichrist film, *The Omen* (1976). 'The gusto with which films like *The Omen* wish for a child's destruction has something deeply suspect about it – might there be a link perhaps between the way in which our more cruel instincts are here being directed against a child, and the disturbing use made of child actors in pornographic films?'[4] Certainly neither film can be said to have the sensitivity of Larry Cohen's film about a 'monster child', *It's Alive* (1974), whose whole thrust is not to compel the father to destroy the child but rather to acknowledge it as his own responsibility.

A similar debate has surfaced in the 1980s with the phenomenal success of Wes Craven's *Nightmare on Elm Street* (1985) and its sequels. Is it not a bit alarming that child-molester Freddie Krueger has become a cult-hero? But Craven's conception seems altogether cannier and more subtle than its predecessors. For one thing, it is established that Freddie is the product of the sins of the parents: he stands as a critique of adult hostilities and repressions rather than an agent of their paedophobia. The Elm Street kids are not like real children when compared with the girl in *The Exorcist* or the boy in *The Omen*. As they fly into dreamland to confront the bogeyman, the

71

material takes on a bizarre flavour of *Peter Pan* as if written by Edgar Allan Poe. These movies also have one quality signally absent from *The Exorcist* and *The Omen*, thus making the films more palatable: a sense of humour. A traumatized teenager stares into a mirror and exclaims in horror: 'I look 20 years old.' A quiet breakfast is abruptly interrupted by a loud scream from upstairs, and the youngest child plaintively asks its mother: 'Mommy, why can't Jessie wake up like everyone else?'

Bourgeois parents unknowingly in the embrace of the Antichrist: Harvey Stevens (left), Lee Remick (centre) and Gregory Peck in Richard Donner's *The Omen* (1976)

CHAPTER FOUR

ARRESTED DEVELOPMENT

I wouldn't want to be growing up now.

(JANE ASHER in *Runners*)

For it was man's sterile curiosity that had deprived him of his innocent life.

(The scientist on the wild child in
François Truffaut's *L'Enfant Sauvage*)

THE theme of this chapter is children in difficulty, the physical and/or psychological growing pains that befall children, which, for many of them, make the passage towards adolescence and adulthood a particularly awkward one. In shaping the theme from their adult perspective, many films inevitably highlight the role of their elders in helping the children towards maturation and equally some disclose how adults are often part of the problem.

Mandy (1952) and *The Miracle Worker* (1962) have been selected as films that are especially interesting and sensitive on the subject of children born with severe physical handicaps, but there are other films on the same theme that warrant some acknowledgement. The Oscar-winning documentary of Lindsay Anderson and Guy Brenton, *Thursday's Children* (1954), observes children and teachers in a school for the deaf in Margate with an admirable lack of sentimentality. Relating the film to Anderson's enthusiasm for the documentaries of Humphrey Jennings, the critic Roy Armes has perceptively summarized its theme as 'the need for the link between feelings and experiences which words provide'[1]: this could equally be applied to *The Miracle Worker*. In dealing with the clash of values between a stern doctor (Burt Lancaster) of a school for mentally retarded children and a humanitarian new assistant (Judy Garland), John Cassavetes' *A Child is Waiting* (1962) does not entirely avoid the dramatic simplifications and emotional

73

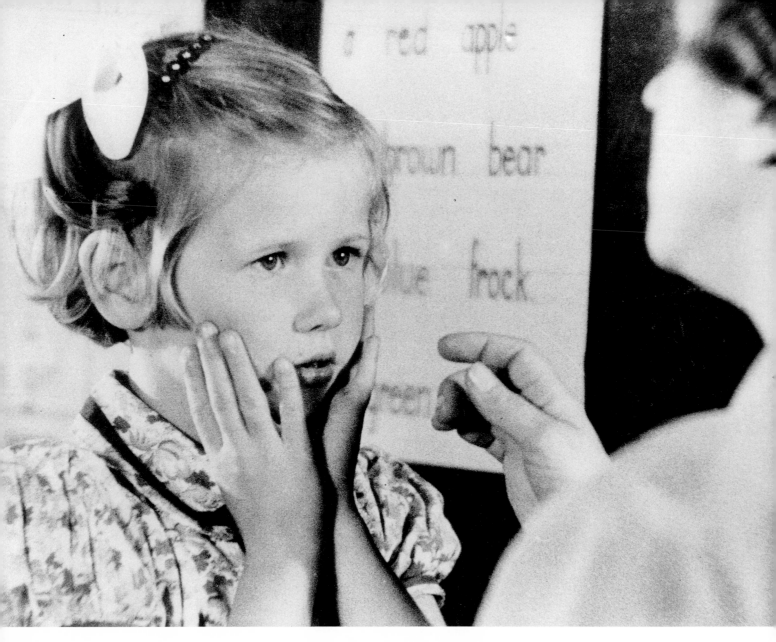

inflation characteristic of the film's producer, Stanley Kramer. It is evading the issue if the boy we are made to identify with is the one closest to 'normality'; it is gilding the lily to have a member of the hospital staff chokingly (rather than matter-of-factly) reveal that his daughter is a mental defective. Nevertheless, the dignity of the performances and the customary edgy reality of Cassavetes' direction make for a rewarding experience. In a similar way, the sentimental nobility of the social worker (Angela Punch-McGregor) in Gil Brealey's *Annie's Coming Out* (1984), as she strives to rescue a disabled but not retarded child from an institution, is offset by other areas of the film that make it an altogether tougher experience than the leading performance might suggest. Like *The Miracle Worker*, it shows the painstaking process of learning how words fit together; the difficult line an adult often has to tread between being passively kind and being actively constructive; and the resilience of even handicapped children in the teeth of adult prejudice. 'Hate made me strong . . .' says the young girl Annie at the beginning of the film, and as things develop we come across attitudes that could credibly have generated the hatred. 'If it was mine, I'd kill it', says the

74

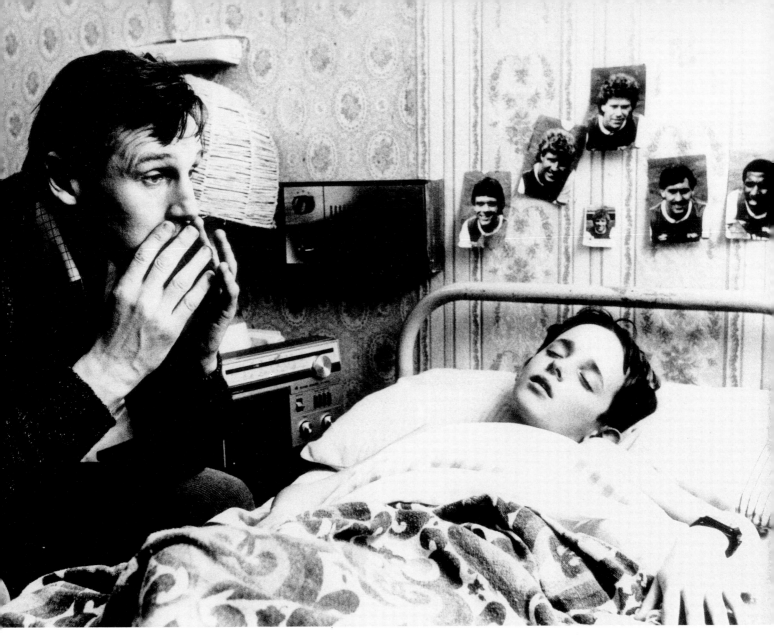

An idealistic priest (Liam Neeson) contemplates the grim future for him and the boy (Hugh O'Conor), whom he has taken from a repressive school. From Colin Gregg's *Lamb* (1987)

social worker's grandmother of Annie, and in the child's hearing. 'She would have to die on open day!' exclaims the ward sister when one of Annie's friends dies. This might seem exaggerated but only to those who have been fortunate enough not to encounter attitudes of sadism that do sometimes linger in hospital wards towards the chronically sick.

Another institution that can harbour sadists, because of the vulnerability and defencelessness of their victims, is the school. As we shall see, the films of Truffaut and Loach touch on those and there are other memorable dramatizations in the same vein. Alf Sjoberg's film of Ingmar Bergman's first script, *Frenzy* (1944), has a shot of a teacher patrolling the empty school corridor that has powerful overtones of a prison movie, and its main character, a teacher (Stig Jarrel) nicknamed 'Caligula', conducts his Latin classes as if they were police interrogations. Jay Peterson's teacher in Michael Dinner's *Catholic Boys* (1984) is another powerful, plausible species of the school sadist, whose only educational achievement is to give the boys a premature sense of injustice. In the same film, prior to a school dance, the boys have to listen to a hellfire sermon that undoubtedly shows the

75

influence of the school scenes of James Joyce's *A Portrait of the Artist as a Young Man*. After watching these films one wonders sometimes how children ever survive for, far from being a haven of education, the school is seen here as the site of bullying and regimentation of attitudes. The director John Hughes seems particularly alert to the problems of young people in this regard. In *Ferris Bueller's Day Off* (1986), he shows a young hero (Matthew Broderick) with enough chutzpah to beat the system and with enough resourcefulness even to tap into the school's computer and improve his grades. In *The Breakfast Club* (1984), he examines the attitudes of the young through five people who have to come into class on a Saturday as school punishment. Slowly the mask of cynicism and hostility towards the authority of teachers and parents slips to reveal a real apprehension of the adult world.

Sometimes, however, the difficulty of growing up is not as overt or external as physical handicap, the tyranny of school or the misunderstanding of parents: it can be much more idiosyncratic, private, personal. In Desmond Davis's *The Uncle* (1967), the cockeyed confusion of the child, Gus, stems from the weirdness of his situation of being a seven-year-old uncle. Davis underlines the theme by frequent distortions of visual scale, suggesting a world that occasionally looks down on Gus, and occasionally suggests a complicity between child and adult. Nevertheless, when Gus adopts a Chaplin disguise the associations are more poignant than comic: he feels freakish and clownish and, like the young Chaplin, old before his time. An equally imaginative, offbeat and neglected movie on a similar theme is Lionel Jeffries's *Baxter!* (1972) about a maladjusted 12-year-old American in London (a superb performance by Scott Jacoby) whose precarious mental world slowly falls apart due to the maladroit ministrations of his inadequate mother (Lynn Carlin) and the death of a beloved friend. With *The Railway Children* (1971) and *The Amazing Mr Blunden* (1972), Jeffries had already shown himself an adept director of children within a limited range of genteel fantasy but *Baxter!*, not entirely successfully but always compellingly, reaches for an altogether greater complexity and richness. It belongs to that group of works, of which Carson McCullers's *The Member of the Wedding* is a supreme fictional example, dealing with the period just before adolescence when childhood is being shed like an old skin but when the child is wondering, half in excitement, half in terror, what she or he might become.

MANDY

(GB 1952: Alexander Mackendrick/US title: *Crash of Silence*)

Handicapped children are often handicapped even more by emotionally disabled adults, who find it difficult to rise to the challenge they set. One of the best films on this theme is *Mandy*, made by one of the cinema's great directors of children, Alexander Mackendrick. Children are always a positive force in his films but their effect seems often destructive, for they alarm their elders and destabilize the certainty of their world, whether it be that of an American businessman in *The Maggie* (1954) or a pirate sea-captain in *A High Wind in Jamaica* (1965)

Mandy (Mandy Miller) is a six-year-old who has been deaf and dumb since birth, although her condition had not been discovered until some time

746·82

The turning point in
Mandy (1952), when the
girl (Mandy Miller)
manages to stir
grandfather (Godfrey
Tearle) from his chess.

afterwards. Cosseted by her parents and grandparents in the grandparents'
polished but petrified middle-class home, she has been allowed to play in
the stony, sterile back-garden but not allowed to come into contact with the
unruly, i.e. 'normal', children who play on the bomb-site beyond the
garden. With her face pressed against the fence that separates her concrete
play-area from the more exciting wasteland, she may look sheltered to the
parents but, to us, she looks more like a prisoner.

After an incident in a park in which Mandy has fought with another
child, her mother Chris (Phyllis Calvert) insists that Mandy must get
accustomed to children of her own age and be sent to a School for the Deaf.
Significantly, this decision about Mandy's future also has profound
implications for the future of Chris's marriage. She is opposed by her
husband, Harry (Terence Morgan), who is supported by his mother
(Marjorie Fielding): his father (Godfrey Tearle) is far too preoccupied with
his games of postal chess – 'the most cerebral of games', as Philip Kemp has

77

noted, 'divorced from even minimal human contact'[2] – to intervene. In an argument about Mandy, Chris accuses Harry's mother of pampering Mandy like 'a spinster with a lapdog', and Harry strikes her. The sound of the slap resounds as strongly as that crashing tray behind Mandy which had first confirmed them in their knowledge that their child was deaf. It is a moment of truth, and clinches Chris's decision. Mandy is enrolled in a special school, under the supervision of Dick Searle (Jack Hawkins).

Under the guidance of the school, whose benevolent hierarchy under the old lady Miss Ellis (Nancy Price) is in such pointed, positive contrast to the stifling sterility of the girl's previous home dominated by her grandparents, Mandy does begin to improve. Paradoxically, as her powers of communication increase, those of the adults seem to diminish. Harry becomes jealous of his displacement from the centre of his wife's and child's universe (for Searle is now more able to help Mandy than he is). He is further tormented by alligations of an affair between Searle and Chris by a vengeful member of the school's board of governors, Ackland (Edward Chapman), who dislikes Searle. If the child is handicapped by her deafness, the adults become equally hamstrung by obstructive pride, power machinations, and by their *symbolic* blindness and deafness.

For example, when Harry first dismisses the school as being unsuitable for Mandy, he is framed by Mackendrick in total shadow. As his wife says later, he might have visited the school but he did not really *see* it. Similarly, many of the conversations in the film take place in a situation where one of the key participants seems only to be half-listening. It happens in an early conversation between husband and wife, and it is the most prominent characteristic of one of Harry's solicitors (Colin Gordon). It is something one notices only subliminally – characters self-preoccupied to the point of near deafness until an extraordinary scene near the end. Preoccupied with his chess game, the grandfather absent-mindedly puts his arm round Mandy; and suddenly Mandy both recognizes the letter 'P' and makes the sound. It is a moment of enormous tension, coming as it does against such a background of adult lethargy, indifference, preoccupation, deafness. We fear the significance of this breakthrough might be missed. Correspondingly, when the grandfather does take notice and takes steps, realizing what might be happening to Mandy and to his son's marriage, the moment is tremendously moving.

There are two particular visual motifs that run through the film, gathering increasing significance. The first is a shot of the back of someone's head. To begin with, this simply signifies deafness. It occurs when Mandy cannot hear the noise being made by her father and mother behind her. We are reminded of it when Chris carries on talking to Miss Ellis whilst the old lady has turned her back on her to reach into her filing cabinet and, from her lack of response, Chris suddenly realizes that she too is deaf. However, as the film proceeds, the motif begins to implicate people who are not literally deaf but who wilfully fail to understand what they hear. So we see the back of the landlady's head as she eavesdrops on Searle and Chris to pass on compromising information about their relationship to Ackland: their joy is actually at Mandy's first word 'Mammy', but she hears it as evidence of adultery. Similarly, when Grandfather intervenes at the end and tells Harry he must decide whether Chris and Searle have been having an affair or been doing their best for Mandy, Mackendrick holds a tense shot of the back of Harry's head: has he really heard and taken in what has been said to him? After a long pause, he turns and declares that he does not believe a word about this so-called 'affair'.

The other motif is one of holding hands. When Chris first visits the school to assess its suitability, a little boy, who can now say his own name, spontaneously takes her hand: it is a gesture that soundlessly seals the bond between Chris and the school. A more disturbing example occurs later. Chris and Harry have been reconciled at a hotel but, on the following morning during breakfast, Harry is disconcerted to find that Searle is coming to see them. 'He is someone who can help Mandy more than *we* can', says Chris, to which Harry replies, gloomily, 'You mean more than I can'. After their previous night of love, Harry's feelings of frustration, jealousy and inadequacy abruptly resurface and the marriage is once again threatened. The moment that crystallizes Harry's jealousy and despair is that in which Mandy instinctively takes Searle's hand: noticing it, Harry makes a quick excuse and leaves.

The final such moment occurs when Mandy has strayed on to the bomb-site to play with the other children. Parenthetically, one should note that the grandfather's breakthrough conversation with his son has been followed by an emotionally liberating forward tracking shot through the open gate that has previously sought to separate Mandy from the outside world. It is a visual correlation to a remark Chris has made when Mandy has uttered her first word – 'It's like seeing the door of a cage open'. The parents come running after her, but then they stop, and Harry takes Chris's hand. It means reconciliation, but it also means loving restraint, checking Chris's instinctive desire to run and protect Mandy. Mandy must come out of the prison they have made for her and make her own way forward.

'Children can be very cruel to each other', the grandmother has said to Chris when opposing the idea of sending Mandy to a school. 'That's life', replies Chris. 'She's got to face up to that whatever happens.' At the end, Mandy is being allowed to face up to that on her own, and the bomb-site is especially expressive and ironic. The rubble, on which the children play, is the legacy from the previous generation and *their* tragic failure to communicate.

Mandy is more than a special case. She is all children, painfully learning the arts of communication in a fearful world, and whose deafness and dumbness are symptoms of the raw potential in all children that the adult world must assist in unlocking and releasing. Indeed, one cannot separate Mandy's condition from the world around her, since her isolation and communication difficulties are shared in a different form by everyone else. Even the teachers, whose dedication contrasts with the self-interest and pomposity of parents, private-eyes and politicians, are nevertheless occasionally prone to self-pity and a lack of perspective. In a different way, the adults are as much in need of teaching as the children. After all, when Mandy cannot talk at one stage in front of her father, it is not her affliction that is restricting her so much as the tension she is picking up from him as he demands proof of the progress Chris claims Mandy is making, yet he is not bright enough to see that. In fact, one could say that the thrust of the film is not so much about the need for Mandy's education as about the need of adults of the post-war generation to re-learn the world around them, in order to make a place fit for children like Mandy to live in. When Mandy returns to her grandparents' home near the end, Mackendrick films it as if it were a readmission into prison, with three entrances one by one closing behind the little girl. The memory of that home lingers on even beyond the marital reconciliation and Mandy's first game with other children. She has made a significant stride forward from out of her silent world, but will she be able to surface from under the values implied by that kindly but disturbingly repressive, life-denying home?

THE MEMBER OF THE WEDDING
(USA 1953: Fred Zinnemann)

The 12-year-old heroine Frankie of Carson McCullers's classic novel *The Member of the Wedding*, is tomboy without portfolio, a self-lacerating hoyden adrift in the vacuum between childhood and puberty. Her anguish stems from the tension between her desire to defy the world and yet her yearning to belong. Her outpourings of inchoate rage and inaccessible dreams are listened to with a mixture of sympathy and exasperation by an effeminate young boy, John Henry, whose puckish humour punctuates and sometimes punctures Frankie's intensity, and by the Negro maid Berenice, who can appraise Frankie's dilemma with humour, irony and, sometimes, with the bitterness of her adult experience.

Adapting his film more from the stage play fashioned from the novel than from the novel itself, Fred Zinnemann also chose to transplant the original Broadway cast: the 25-year-old Julie Harris as Frankie, Brandon DeWilde as John Henry and Ethel Waters as Berenice. It is hard to imagine their performances being bettered. It was Julie Harris's screen debut and she once told me that her main fear in the film was giving a performance that was too big for the screen. In fact, director and actress calculate the projection of the part with some subtlety. All theatricality cannot be removed from the performance because Frankie is a theatrical person, given to self-dramatization. Her loudness has to be retained, because that is a dimension of her dilemma: no one really listens to her – her brother, her father, even at times Berenice. (The deafness of adults to the pain of children is to have a tragic outcome in the fate of poor John Henry, who is ignored by Berenice at precisely the time he most needs help.) If Julie Harris's performance is big, the reason is that Frankie *is* big for her age, emphasizing her sense of freakishness and alienation; she *does* use words that are too big for her, relishing their sound without understanding their meaning; and above all, she is trying to grow up too fast. She ventures into the adult world before she (or the world) is ready. On the first occasion, she tries to climb into her brother's wedding car and is bodily pulled out. On the second, she leaves home and ventures into the town, and the adult world is vividly presented as a discordant and frightening confusion of sights and sounds – sinister dark alleys, overheard marital squabbles, threatening masculinity – leading

Frankie (Julie Harris, in the car) wants to accompany her brother (Arthur Frank) and his new bride (Nancy Gates) on their honeymoon. From *The Member of the Wedding* (1953)

to Frankie's flight (when no one is chasing her) from darkness into morning and back to the world she knows.

The film's sense of confinement is attributable to its theatrical origins but it also seems highly appropriate to Frankie's sense of her own entrapment. 'It was better to be in a jail where you could bang the walls,' she feels 'than in a jail you could not see.' She feels locked inside her own character and longs for escape into another identity, frequently changing her name – Frankie, Frances, F. Jasmine – as if it will magically confer on her a different personality. She feels suffocated by her enviroment, by the 'empty, ugly house', which seems to correspond in personality to what she feels about herself. In Julie Harris's performance, Frankie is always picking at herself: admonishing, improving, restless, and as spiky as the splinters she keeps getting in her feet; and everything about her appearance (her rough crew-cut, her grubby elbows) betokens a personality at odds with itself. If she is a tomboy, she is a tormented one, played wholly without cuteness or sentimentality. She longs to look feminine, but the image of elegance she presents is incongruous, like her choice of dress for her brother's wedding

81

whose inappropriateness for her is colourfully summarized by Berenice: 'I ain't accustomed to seeing human Christmas trees in August.'

Frankie's most intense dream is her fantasy of accompanying her brother and his wife after their wedding: 'This coming Sunday when my brother and his bride leave this town, I'm going with the two of them to Winter Hill. And after that to whatever place they will ever go. I love the two of them so much and we belong together. I love the two of them so much because they are the *we* of me.' She will not accompany them, of course, and her rejection will be a humiliating but important stage in her coming to terms with herself, in a way discovering the 'me' of 'we'.

The 'we of me' speech – one of the highlights of the film, radiantly shot and acted – has been triggered by Frankie's listening to the sound of Berenice's foster brother, Honey (James Edwards), as he plays his horn. Honey is a minor character but, thematically, important to the whole structure, as he puts Frankie's problems into perspective. Just as Frankie feels an unwanted stranger in her world, so does Honey in his. On the night when Frankie tries to escape from her world so Honey tries to escape from his (after he has accidentally run over a white man in his car). Both Frankie and Honey have similar bouts of violent rage that Berenice has to control. Both of them feel excluded but the difference is that, whereas Frankie's struggles are with herself, Honey's, as a Negro, are with a whole social structure.

This might be the reason that, at the end of the film, Zinnemann chooses to stay with Berenice rather than with Frankie. Her heavy, motionless melancholy in that last scene, the result of her self-reproach for the death of John Henry, casts a doleful shadow across Frankie's new-found stability. Frankie's agonies have been transient growing pains, but adult pain lasts. 'Your road is already strange to me now', Berenice tells Frankie, and the weight of her sadness (disclosed in her mannerism of humming to herself when her heart is breaking) dominates the final scene, setting Frankie's new enthusiasm and adjustment against Berenice's enduring isolation and emptiness.

As a postscript to *The Member of the Wedding*, it is necessary to mention Claude Miller's 1985 film, *L'Effrontée* (*An Impudent Girl*), which offers a virtual reprise of McCullers's situations but also a fresh French perspective on them. It is also about the growing pains of a young girl, Charlotte (Charlotte Gainsbourg), who similarly has a sickly young friend (female not male), a sympathetic maid (white, not Negro) and an elder brother whom she wants to accompany on his travels (though he is going camping, not getting married). She even has Frankie's horrendous dress sense, which makes her, in the words of the screenplay (and this is surely the movie's most overt homage to *Member of the Wedding*), look like a Christmas tree in July. Like Frankie, she too has a groping encounter with a predatory male (Jean Philippe Ecoffey), who is characterized with a great deal more sympathy and depth than in Zinnemann's film. Charlotte also tries to escape from the confines of her world, in her case through a fortuitous friendship with a rich and talented concert pianist of her own age, Clara (Clothilde Boudon).

Nevertheless, Miller's film does inhabit a different sort of imaginative world. The class tensions of *L'Effrontée* are completely different from the

The tomboy and the concert pianist: Charlotte Gainsbourg (left) and Clothilde Boudon (right) in Claude Miller's *An Impudent Girl* (1985)

racial sub-themes of *Member*, this being most strikingly signalled in the films' musical soundtracks – Mozart and Mendelssohn prominent in Miller, blues and hymns prominent in Zinnemann. If Frankie's world has an American South Gothicism that gradually scales itself down into the manageably mundane, Charlotte's in *L'Effrontée* has a naturalistic base that imperceptibly moves to a magical level, with her rich friend's house becoming charged with the atmosphere of a fairy palace. On the whole, it is a lighter, less intense, less operatic film than Zinnemann's, helped by the fact that, in Miller's film, Charlotte's young friend Lulu (Julie Glenn) survives her illness, and that Miller's 'impudent girl' is played by an actress of the right age, and beautifully too. This is intended as no disrespect to Julie Harris nor to Zinnemann's film, but just a definition of the different kind of film experience Miller offers from what superficially might appear the same material. Unlike Frankie Adams, Charlotte does not see herself as a 'freak': just a normal shy girl going through a depressingly typical pre-adolescent period of confusion and despair. Frankie was an exceptionally difficult 12-year-old. Charlotte simply reminds us that 12 can be an exceptionally difficult age to be.

THE 400 BLOWS – LES QUATRE CENTS COUPS
(France 1959 : François Truffaut)

Having escaped from a reformatory, a young boy, Antoine Doinel (Jean-Pierre Léaud), runs towards the sea in a gesture of freedom; then stops and turns to face the camera, at which point the image freezes. It is a many-layered shot with numerous resonances: isolating the boy in his solitude; flattening him into a still photograph that recalls the police ID picture of him to categorize him as 'delinquent'; ending the film on a point of stasis, another bid for freedom having come to a dead end; and also ending the film on a question mark, the boy's gaze directly into the camera seeming to implicate every audience in his fate and in the future of boys like him. It is one of the most eloquent last shots in film history, and the freeze-frame ending has never been the same since.

In an interview in *Arts* magazine, (29 April-5 May, 1959), Truffaut said: 'I made my film on this crisis that specialists call by the nice name of "juvenile identity crisis", which shows up in the form of four precise disturbances: the onset of puberty; an emotional weaning on the part of the parents; a desire for independence; and an inferiority complex. Each one of these four features leads to revolt and the discovery that a certain sort of injustice exists.' Antoine Doinel's problem is not that he is a juvenile delinquent: it is that he is 13. He is in the troublesome void between childhood and adulthood, where he is still being treated as a child at the same time as growing painfully aware of the hypocrisies of the adult world. His father (Albert Remy) stresses honesty whilst also openly admiring a colleague who is fiddling his tax returns. His mother (Claire Maurier) only affects intimacy and friendship towards Antoine when she wants him to conceal from his father his knowledge of her affair with her boss. As she talks to him of the need for people to have secrets, Truffaut delays the reaction shot of Antoine to allow us to experience her disclosures as Antoine does, where sympathy and interest gradually give way to cynicism as the obviousness of her strategy becomes apparent. It is affectation not affection, a ruse to buy Antoine's silence, a mother's love perceived as calculated emotional blackmail.

Life at school and, later, reformatory offer a dreary routine of uniformity and punishment. The film has numerous images implying imprisonment and claustrophobia as adult values are scrutinized from the perspective of the powerless adolescent, who is himself barely allowed to exist and has few real opportunities to strike back. One such opportunity occurs when Antoine is being berated by a schoolmaster for suspected truancy and, on the spur of the moment, invents a story that his mother has died. It is a shocking untruth, but one that we both relish and understand. It momentarily embarrasses an unpleasant authoritarian, who is suddenly stopped in his tracks, his certainties undermined. Also it is a recognizable, authentic, even sympathetic strategy of survival. Antoine is not simply lying but also protecting himself, thinking desperately of something that will delay, if not avoid, his inevitable punishment. All the more shocking, then, is the moment when Nemesis arrives. His parents come to the school and Antoine is struck by his father in full view of his schoolfellows.

Like many children experiencing difficulty in adapting to the world of school or outside (the boy in *Kes* will be the same), Antoine seems accident-prone. He is always in trouble not because he is inordinately bad but because he always gets caught. He is finally sent to a reformatory for stealing a typewriter he was actually trying to return, having found it far too cumbersome an object to serve any useful purpose as stolen property. In Antoine, perhaps more than in any other cinematic character, Truffaut has established the prototype of child as scapegoat, and childhood as the ultimate period of victimization. In this respect, Truffaut can be regarded as the cinema's Dickens and it is probably no accident that, when the hero of Truffaut's *Fahrenheit 451* (1966) secretly sits down to read in a society where books are forbidden, the text he chooses is the opening of one of the great novels of childhood, Dickens's *David Copperfield*: 'Whether I shall turn out to be the hero of my own life, or whether that station will be held by anybody else, these pages must show. To begin my life with the beginning of my life, I record that I was born (as I have been informed and believe) on Friday at 12 o'clock at night. It was remarked that the clock began to strike, and I began to cry, simultaneously.'

Les Quatre Cents Coups is regarded by many as the definitive film about childhood, and the reason for this seems to lie in the intensity with which Truffaut identifies with Antoine and the precocious cinematic skill with which that intensity is conveyed to an audience. This precosity is actually a consequence of Truffaut's sensitivity as a film critic and fruitful application

Stealing the typewriter
in *The 400 Blows* (1959)

of this sensibility to his feature film début. Crucially, Truffaut recognized that a subjective film was actually the opposite of the subjective camera since, when the camera is substituted for a given person, it is impossible to identify with him. The subjective film is that film in which the actor's gaze meets that of the audience and we are made to identify with Antoine because the film concentrates so much on his face. For example, his ride on the merry-go-round is mainly conveyed in facial close-up, a treasurable time when he feels free and the oppressive world is turned upside down but where he is actually being whirled around in a tightly limited circle by forces outside of himself. His interview by the prison psychiatrist is filmed entirely from the point of view of a close-up of Antoine's face – very immediate and engaging but implicitly commenting also on the impersonality of the interrogator, who symbolizes the detached indifference to Antoine of the institutionalized adult world.

Truffaut had one word for this kind of subjectivity in film: 'Hitchcockian'. He knew that Hitchcock was unrivalled at forging an identification between character and audience: indeed, at the time Truffaut was making his film, Hitchcock was preparing his ultimate example of subjective filmmaking, the opening 40 minutes of *Psycho* (1960), in which we are compelled to share the terrified and terrifying company of Janet Leigh's guilty secretary. Hitchcock's influence can be felt in the point-of-view travelling shots of Paris by night as Antoine is being transported by police van (Jean Constantine's mocking music echoing Antoine's melancholy disorientation). It is also noticeable in the fingerprinting scene in the police station, in which Antoine's identity seems to be drained out of him as remorselessly as Henry Fonda's in a similar scene in Hitchcock's *The Wrong Man* (1957). Another key influence was undoubtedly Nicholas Ray, the cinema's most impassioned champion of the young outsider in films such as *They Live by Night* (1948) and *Rebel Without a Cause* (1955), which had made a deep impression on the young Truffaut. In certain details of his film, Truffaut undoubtedly evokes *Rebel Without a Cause* – it is hard to watch Antoine's father in a pinafore without thinking of Jim Backus's similarly emasculated father figure in *Rebel* – and Truffaut's wonderful tribute to James Dean in 1956 seems almost a foretaste of his presentation of Antoine: 'Today's young people are represented completely in James Dean, less for the reasons that are usually given – violence, sadism, frenzy, gloom, pessimism and cruelty – than for other reasons that are infinitely more simple and everyday: morality, continual fantasizing, a moral purity not related to the prevailing morality but in fact stricter, the adolescent's eternal taste for experience, intoxication, pride and the sorrow at feeling "outside"....'[3]

The other factor that explains the immediacy of the film's impact is probably this: that the boy is, or will become, François Truffaut. Like Antoine, Truffaut had a troubled childhood and a spell in a reformatory. Like Truffaut, Antoine has an artistic personality, reading Balzac by candlelight and stealing cinema stills that seduce his imagination: Harriet Andersson at her most sensual in Bergman's *Summer with Monika* (1952). (A variation of that will recur in the mysterious dream sequence of Truffaut's 1973 classic about film-making, *Day for Night*, in which the director, played by Truffaut, fragmentedly remembers stealing a cinema poster of *Citizen*

Kane.) However, the story also becomes that of Jean-Pierre Léaud. Antoine becomes a mixture of Truffaut's shyness and Leaud's cockiness, and Truffaut will find that he cannot leave this character alone, constructing a sentimental education through subsequent films in which Antoine's story-telling gifts and difficulties with women as an adult clearly have their roots in his troubled childhood. The career of Truffaut owed a lot to this character and, with characteristic generosity, he acknowledged the debt by dedicating his most intense study of the adult/child relationship, *L'Enfant Sauvage* (1969) to his former 'pupil', Jean-Pierre Léaud.

Truffaut's interest in the theme of childhood was to be one of the constant factors of his work. It no doubt owed something to his enormous admiration for classic French treatments of the theme, like Jean Vigo's movie *Zero de Conduite* (1932) or Jean Cocteau's novel *Les Enfants Terribles*, for Truffaut, as much as anyone, used celluloid as a means of paying homage to his cultural heroes. Yet it is clear that the theme appealed to him anyway. In *Jules et Jim* (1961), a shot of Jim and the little girl Sabine laughingly rolling down a grassy slope is one of the cinema's most entrancing images of childhood joy; in *Small Change* (1975), childhood is proffered as a state of grace and continual covert rebellion; in *The Green Room* (1978) a handicapped child stands for the troubled and traumatized new generation following the First World War. In his criticism too, Truffaut wrote with special passion about childhood, excoriating what he saw as the suspect fantasy of *The Red Balloon*, writing with infinite delicacy of the childlike genius of Chaplin. It was smart of Steven Spielberg to cast him as the scientist with a child's sense of wonder in *Close Encounters of the Third Kind* (1977); and although his death at the age of 54 was untimely, Truffaut as a venerable veteran is a difficult concept to imagine. As the supreme baby-faced cineaste, Truffaut would no doubt have quoted John Derek's philosophy from a film he much admired, Nicholas Ray's *Knock on Any Door* (1949): 'Live fast, die young, and have a good-looking corpse.'

THE MIRACLE WORKER
(USA 1962: Arthur Penn)

Although *The Miracle Worker* is famous as the play and film that most effectively dramatizes the story of Helen Keller's victory over deafness and blindness, the title is significant for it actually draws attention not to the child but to her teacher, Annie Sullivan. Contrast this with thematically similar films like *Mandy*, *L'Enfant Sauvage* or Gil Brealey's 1984 Australian drama, *Annie's Coming Out*, in which, although the role of the teacher is important, the title implies that the essential focus is the child. Another curiosity about the title of *The Miracle Worker* is that it might be intended ironically. Annie Sullivan does not really work miracles: she just works very hard. Also what she does is to rediscover a faculty in the child that Helen's mother has first unlocked when Helen was six months old, before the illness that robbed her of sight and hearing: namely the ability to connect the word 'water' with the matter running through her hands, and to say the word. From this, all understanding will flow.

As a film by Arthur Penn, *The Miracle Worker* has a number of interesting and characteristic features (and it is obviously a work he felt close to, for he

Making contact: Anne Bancroft as Annie Sullivan (left) and Patty Duke as Helen Keller (right) in *The Miracle Worker* (1962)

had directed William Gibson's script also on television and on stage). As *The Left-Handed Gun* (1958) and *Bonnie and Clyde* (1967) are films examining the reality behind a legend, so too does *The Miracle Worker*. It shows the heroic Helen Keller (Patty Duke) to be originally an unruly child – more petty tyrant than pitiable tot – and it demystifies the notion of Annie Sullivan (Anne Bancroft) as an example of noble self-sacrifice. Learning and teaching in this instance become a battle of blood, sweat and tears.

'What is it to you?' asks the patriarchal head of the household, Captain Keller (Victor Jory), puzzled by Annie's obsessive, almost demonic, determination ('If God did not mean Helen to see or speak,' says Annie, 'I mean her to'). The answer to that is complex. On one level, Annie is fascinated by Helen because she recognizes in her elements of herself that she had either to channel constructively or overcome. Like Helen, as a child Annie was blind and still needs her dark glasses to protect her from the light. Typically, she has turned this to her strategic advantage, discomfiting antagonists like Captain Keller by using her glasses as a disconcerting shield against enquiring eyes. Just as Helen was once in danger of being sent to an asylum, Annie and her brother, Jamie, had spent time in such a place: it had, she says, made her strong. Above all, she senses in Helen a quality that had lifted *her* out of her darkness: an insatiable curiosity and a desire to learn. At an important stage she can exploit that to overcome Helen's temporary hatred of her. She feigns to teach a black child her finger-alphabet in preference to Helen, and Helen angrily pushes the child away and joins in with Annie. (It is an effective little cameo in another way: given her lowly situation, Annie could not have treated a *white* child in that manner, and the incident is a discreet reminder of the many different *social* as well as physical ways in which a child's natural development can be arrested.)

Yet, there is more to Annie's determination than recognition of some kinship with her child-charge. Annie's treatment of Helen – the power it gives her, the time she takes, her insistence on the child's dependence on her – is a means of gaining ascendancy in a situation where, as a single governess in a male-dominated tradionalist household of the American South in the late nineteenth century, she would ordinarily have very little status. Helen becomes Annie's instrument of influence and growing self-esteem and, significantly, it is only after she has succeeded with Helen that she can tell the child that she loves her. Furthermore her behaviour towards Helen is an implicit challenge to Captain Keller's authority in his home, one that he cannot counter if he really cares for the child as much as he says. (It is a variation of the father's dilemma in *Mandy*.) It is also a means of supplanting Mrs Keller as the child's 'mother'. When she rocks Helen to sleep on her knee by crooning 'Hush little baby, don't you cry', Annie is becoming Helen's mother by default, as it were, and without the pain of childbirth.

Although her motives are complicated, this does not devalue the beneficial effect of Annie's teaching of Helen. Prior to her arrival, Helen was at best an indulged pet and at worst a wild animal. The opening shot of her, as she tangles herself in some washing hanging from a line, conveys the sense of someone trying vainly to find her way through a maze. Later on, when Annie has Helen to herself, there is a scene when Annie gives her an egg to hold and a chick breaks through the shell. The wider resonances of the scene are clear enough – Annie is similarly trying to liberate Helen from her shell of physical and mental darkness – but the most striking thing is the look on Helen's face when the light strikes her. For the first time we see an expression of tenderness, which Annie, in her frustrating endeavour to get Helen to make the connection between the objects she feels and the words she is spelling out on her fingers, barely notices. Yet it is perhaps this moment that, more than any other thus far in the film, expresses the ideal of teaching: education as wonder, as an opening up of the world, a breaking through of the shells of ignorance and incomprehension, a bringing of light into darkness, eloquence into muteness.

If Annie is less attentive to Helen's reaction at this stage than she might be, a possible reason is that there is another aspect to her charge that torments her. It seems that Annie has an obscure feeling of guilt over the death of her younger brother, Jamie, whom she feels she might have abandoned in her own determination to get ahead. Penn sketches this in shadowy flashback, introducing fragments of tormented memory at times of emotional crisis for Annie. It is one more bond between her and Helen, who also has a brother Jamie but who is also dependent on Annie's strength. This time she will not give up.

What particularly characterizes Annie's determination is her capacity to absorb and administer violence, which in the film, is prolonged and distressing and completely demolishes any sentimental reading of the Annie Sullivan/Helen Keller relationship. Some critics felt an element of sadism in Annie's treatment of Helen, particularly in the epic battle in the dining room after which, as Annie puts it, 'the room's a wreck but her napkin is folded'. In fact, Helen has already been violent towards Annie, breaking a tooth by cracking her in the face with a doll, so Annie knows that simple kindness will not do. Something more fundamental is involved, however. The Kellers want a house-trained child: Annie wants to unlock her intelligence. Her refusal to pet her is a mark of her respect. The brusqueness and occasional brutality are really part of the treatment; pity would only get in the way. Also, unlike the Kellers, who are prepared to tolerate anything for a quiet life, Annie has energy enough for the task. Maybe energy is the key. Whereas the Keller family wants to subdue Helen's energy into socialized conventionality, Annie wants to discipline that dynamism and turn it in a direction that will open up her world.

'I have always equated the American temperament with the kinetic temperament', said Arthur Penn on one occasion. 'I like kinetic behaviour; I think that's good for cinema. Kinetic-Cinema: the two words have the same source.'[4] The aggresion bubbling through *The Miracle Worker* does seem emblematic of a specifically American vitality. Contrast it with the repressed restraint of the British *Mandy* or the clinical coolness of the French *L'Enfant Sauvage*. *The Miracle Worker* is an emotional powerhouse, sensual rather than cerebral, in which the deepest emotional contact comes through touch. (D. H. Lawrence would have loved it.) Everything builds to that overwhelming moment when Helen, feeling the water from the pump splashing over her hands, at last understands what Annie has been trying to teach her. She says 'Wahwah' (the word she first uttered when she was only six months old) and spells out the word W-A-T-E-R. Annie's fingers at last have become the current to energize Helen's eyes and ears. The dam of knowledge bursts.

KES

(GB 1969: Ken Loach)

Kes is a tragic love story about a schoolboy Billy Casper (David Bradley) and a kestrel that he finds, adopts, nurtures and trains. Formerly Billy has been involved in acts of delinquency and petty theft: the hawk has had the effect of socializing him, or at least keeping him out of trouble. 'He never knocks around with anybody else . . . he's mad over it', says one schoolboy when the teacher, Mr Farthing (Colin Welland), is pressing Billy to talk about something that has happened to him and the subject of the kestrel is raised. He begins to talk hesitantly about the bird to the class, but as he warms to his subject and he feels the attention, absorption and even exhilaration of his audience, his spirit takes flight. It is the working-class schoolboy's equivalent of Henry V's speech at Agincourt. Momentarily he is king of the classroom, imparting information, answering questions, inspiring by example.

It is a beautifully acted, written and directed scene, but it also owes much of its impact to its context. It is not only the first time in the film that Billy has found his voice, but also the first time he has discovered an audience that *listens*. It makes a telling contrast to the scene that has just preceded it in the office of the headmaster, who has launched a tirade against his young miscreants – 'Yours is the generation that never listens' – but who himself does not listen to an innocent youngster who has merely brought a message and who is about to be included in the punishment. Also Billy's classroom speech is in the context of a lesson about fact and fiction, a detail that is a quick reminder of the celebrated opening school scene of Dickens's *Hard Times*: 'Now what I want is Facts. Teach these boys and girls nothing but Facts. Facts alone are wanted in life. Plant nothing else and root out everything else.' Like *Hard Times*, *Kes* is an indictment of an educational system tending to uniformity, utilitarianism and a mechanization of the

Symbol of freedom: the boy (David Bradley) and his kestrel friend in *Kes*

human spirit. What Billy has to say in this school lesson contains its own implicit lesson about schooling, and a system that restricts rather than releases potential. Remember that this school scene, in which Billy discloses the most fundamental interest of his life, is taking place only two weeks before he is due to leave.

Without straining for symbolic significance, the film invites all kinds of inferences from Billy's relationship with the kestrel and his devotion to it. In the same way that the pigeons he cares for suggest a gentler side to Marlon Brando's hero in *On the Waterfront* (1954), so too does the kestrel suggest a sensitivity in Billy quite unperceived by family and teachers. Whereas Billy previously sought relief in his comics from the oppressive industrial greyness around him ('I'm not goin' down pit' is his one constant refrain), now he finds it in the kestrel's natural grace, a contrast that places *Kes* firmly in the tradition of English Romanticism and particularly in the tradition of an anti-industrial work of art such as D. H. Lawrence's *The Rainbow*. The flight of the kestrel not only somehow expresses Billy's rebellion against the bleakly limited future into which his soul is being wedged by his elders, but also offers Billy a glimpse of the existence of another kind of life, one that is instinctual and free. It represents Billy's mute, inexpressible aspirations, and the brutal killing of it by his brother (because Billy has failed to place a winning bet for him at the betting shop) implies the death of something more than just the bird. Billy finds it in the rubbish-bin finally, a brutal metaphor for the fate of his aspirations and for the social scrap-heap that his schooling has implied is all he is fit for. In the novel Hines strains for tragic eloquence in the final pages (I am reminded of F. R. Leavis's criticism of the final pages of *The Rainbow*, as if Lawrence were looking for somewhere to stop): the film's terseness is much more effective. Billy buries it quietly – the burial perhaps of his hopes and certainly of a grief inside him too deep for any words.

The killing of the kestrel brings together two other sub-themes of the film that have been a disturbing undercurrent in Billy's life: violence and injustice, at school and at home. Billy is subjected to constant physical threats from his brutish elder brother, Jud (Freddie Fletcher). A counterpart of Jud appears in the form of the sports master (Brian Glover), also blond and loutish. He recalls Woody Allen's aphorism in *Annie Hall* (1977): 'Those who can't do, teach: those who can't teach, teach gym.' He also shows a relish for bullying disturbingly close to sadism. Mr Farthing's status as the most sympathetic adult in the film is confirmed when he rescues Billy from being bullied by a bigger boy. School and family are similarly implicated in the theme of injustice. The unfairness of school life is underlined at a number of points in the film: when a boy is randomly picked out from a pack as the scapegoat culprit who has been caught coughing during assembly; when Billy is punished for understandably dozing off during school hours; and unforgettably in that lingering close-up of a smartly dressed schoolboy in the headmaster's office, tears forming in his eyes after being caned when he was only delivering a message, and his only protest being a single word, 'Sir . . .'. Equally moving as a concise image of life's unfairness is the scene at home after Billy has discovered Kes in the dustbin and demands that his mother give Jud 'a good hiding'. 'What you goin' to do to him? I want you to *do* summat to him.' It is a desperate shout from a vulnerable generation for some form of adult authority to administer some form of appropriate justice. But no help is forthcoming.

Perhaps this summary gives the impression that *Kes* is a more depressing film than it actually is, though I do think it is the equal of such neo-realist masterpieces as *Bicycle Thieves* and *Umberto D* in giving the texture of impoverished lives and evoking sympathy for the desperate situation of the insulted and injured in our society. If this drama-doc., ciné-vérité method has its limitations, it is that it reproduces the external world so authentically and naturalistically that it implies a kind of status quo. Far from converting people, it might even confirm them in their prejudices. *Kes* is so fierce in its indictment of the assembly-line attitude to education (I like the detail of the employment officer's getting Billy's name wrong simply because Billy has entered out of alphabetical order) that it could be interpreted as a diatribe against comprehensive education, which I doubt was the intention.

The scenes involving Jud, particularly his night out and his unlikely prowling of the school grounds in search of Billy, are amongst the film's weakest and least convincing. Against that one can applaud the film's undoubted improvement of the novel's structure by shifting the order of its sequences, and the wonderful humour of the school football sequence, with its parody *Match of the Day* captions, its air of fantasy, and where for once calculated injustice comes unstuck. The games teacher's blatant attempts to rig the match still fail through Billy's intervention (his incompetence as a goalkeeper). It has the equivalent feeling of Antoine's small victory over the teacher in *The 400 Blows*, but will similarly be followed by a blow directed at the boy.

Where the film is strongest is in its depiction of an inarticulate boy's soul. Played with a perkily matter-of-fact, beaten-but-not-defeated air by David Bradley, Billy is a lad who cannot define his own aspirations and what one might call his own spirituality but who briefly finds a kestrel to express them for him. Other Loach films like *Black Jack* (1979), with its Dickensian sense of social injustice, and *Looks and Smiles* (1982), with its desolate look at youth unemployment, show a similar concern for young people. Yet none has the eloquence or magic of *Kes*.

THE WILD CHILD – L'ENFANT SAUVAGE
(France 1969: François Truffaut)

'From Romulus and Remus through Mowgli and Tarzan', said François Truffaut in publicity releases for *L'Enfant Sauvage*, 'men have continually been fascinated by tales of beast children. It may be that in these stories of abandoned infants, reared by wolves, bears or apes, they see a symbol of the extraordinary destiny of our race. Or it may be simply that they harbour a secret hankering after a natural existence.' Partially stimulated by Truffaut's admiration of a stage production he had seen of *The Miracle Worker*, Truffaut's tale of a 'beast child' is based on a true story of a wild boy who was discovered and captured in a forest in France in 1798. Truffaut himself takes the role of the scientist Dr Itard, who, as an experiment to 'determine the intelligence of a child deprived of education and human contact', undertakes to bring up the boy with his housekeeper in his home in the country. The role of the boy, Victor, is played, remarkably well, by Jean-Pierre Cargol.

The material can by taken on many levels. Because of Nestor Almendros's 'primitive' black-and-white photography and Truffaut's deployment of devices more common in the silent cinema, such as the frequent use of iris shots, the film could be taken as an allegory of the childhood of the cinema. In a way, like Victor, its expression was initially wild, reckless, formally primitive and yet still inventive: it was also, like Victor's, a language of gesture and embarking on a voyage of discovery. ('What fascinates me', says Itard at one stage, 'is that everything he does, he does for the first time.') Gradually Victor learns a discipline; he acquires speech. But is there also (as some historians feel about the cinema's transition to the sound era) some loss of vitality? Even in an eighteenth-century story, the ciné-literacy of Truffaut cannot be repressed. Possibly accidentally, the structure of the film – an adult's adoption of a stray child, his teaching him what he knows, a despairing period when the child has gone, the elation of reunion – has a strong similarity to one of the silent films Truffaut most admired, Chaplin's *The Kid* (1921). A scene where the child plays freely out in the open whilst adults behind the window decide his fate seems, in its staging, consciously to imitate the crucial childhood scene of *Citizen Kane* (1941).

Another reason why Truffaut might have been drawn to the material is an element of autobiography: a wild boy whose excesses are tamed and disciplined by the stern compassion of a master – in Truffaut's case, his mentor André Bazin. (Truffaut in turn felt he played the same role in the life of Jean-Pierre Léaud.) Ultimately the themes of the film are far more wide-ranging than personal or cinematic reference. At its most basic level, *L'Enfant Sauvage* is an allegory of childhood itself, the wild boy a symbol of the child in its most natural state, privileged to sustain innocence, instinct, vitality a little longer than the norm before necessary educative and social forces overtake him.

The period of the film – the point of transition between the eighteenth and nineteenth centuries, from the Age of Reason to the Age of Romanticism – is undoubtedly significant. The scientist Itard is the ultimate rational man, a prototype of eighteenth-century classicism. Victor, on the other hand, is a child of nature, whose spirit has not yet been stifled by interiors (even in Itard's house, he habitually takes his water to the window from which he can view nature) and who is a kind of precursor of Romanticism. What takes place between them can be seen as the eternal struggle in childhood between the inclination to individual freedom and yet the necessity of social integration.

Truffaut's sensitivity and ambivalence towards this theme has a curious effect on the film's tone. Unlike, say, the progress of Mandy, or that of Helen Keller in *The Miracle Worker*, the more Victor learns, the more melancholy the film seems to become. There are several reasons for this. One is the film's vision of childhood, which is essentially a melancholy one: a rebellion that is doomed to fail. Connected with this is Itard's growing realization of what he has taken on. 'You turn all his pleasures into exercises', says the housekeeper to him at one stage. His method of discovering whether Victor has a moral sense is the cruel one of punishing him unjustly. It is true that

François Truffaut as teacher and scientist (right); Jean-Pierre Cargol as pupil and experiment (left). From *L'Enfant Sauvage* (1969)

Itard becomes a sort of substitute parent to Victor, for his part acquiring a son without having to go through the process of finding a wife, yet in his behaviour symbolizing a notion of parenthood as benevolent education, a process of socialization. At the same time, he cannot suppress a sense of loss as Victor's exuberance stabilizes and he discovers sorrow. Perhaps even sadder is that Itard's recognition of this cannot restrain his obsession. After Victor has come back, signalling his return by knocking on the window through which he has earlier escaped (perhaps he unconsciously recognizes the inevitability of social integration, by now asking to be let back in), Itard is overjoyed, but his, and the film's, final line is: 'Tomorrow we'll resume our work'.

CHAPTER FIVE

THE CHILDREN ARE WATCHING US

I'd like to tell a story about how we have to forgive our parents.

(WILLIAM INGE on the writing of *Splendour in the Grass*)

'How come you have two fathers?'
'Just lucky, I guess.'

(*Paris, Texas*)

IF, as the saying goes, youth is wasted on the young, it has to be said that maturity often fares little better in the hands of the adult. Whereas the previous chapter concerned children in trouble, a state that their elders were either unequipped to help with or sometimes even to blame for, this chapter focuses on adults in difficulty and the impact this has on their children. The problems range from poverty (*Bicycle Thieves*) to politics (*A World Apart*), where adult failures rebound to affect the new generation. The problems can also range from paternal petulance, as in *Meet Me in St Louis*, to the complex stirrings of passion, which the children observe either with detachment (*Days of Heaven*) or derision (*Les Mistons*).

'If kids had their way,' says the plumber in *The 5,000 Fingers of Dr T*, 'practically no parents would be born at all.' In a lot of cases, you can feel the kids have a point. Parents are a lot of trouble, particularly when doing things for adult reasons that nevertheless cause children to suffer – like, for example, divorce. Speaking from personal experience Steven Spielberg has said that, when two parents are contemplating divorce and they have children, it is at first an abstract word that children cannot understand: then suddenly it assumes an appallingly concrete form. Inspired by this Spielberg observation, David Pirie's script for Rob Walker's BBC TV film, *Wild Things* (1988), is an imaginative projection of the way children perceive divorce, the way they weigh the pros and cons, and the way they

size up any potential new step-parent. In more conventional cinematic terms, so too is Alan Parker's *Shoot the Moon* (1982), from a fine script by Bo Goldman. Robert Benton's *Kramer vs Kramer* (1979) is probably the film that makes the biggest emotional meal of this theme, though less to explore the impact on the child than to celebrate the domestic resourcefulness of noble dad (Dustin Hoffman) who towards the end is cracking an egg for breakfast as if he were splitting an atom for mankind. More cynically convincing about adult behaviour under stress is *Irreconcilable Differences* (1983), where a young girl (Drew Barrymore) tries to obtain a divorce from her parents (Ryan O'Neal and Shelley Long) because she feels they are unworthy of her; and Robert M. Young's *Rich Kids* (1980), where the kids are invited for a meal at their favourite restaurant, partly to cushion the blow when their parents announce their impending divorce, and partly as an adult ruse to avoid a scene.

If divorce is one source of difficulty between parents and children,

A schoolgirl plots revenge against her domineering teacher (Maggie Smith) in *The Prime of Miss Jean Brodie* (1969)

98

Father and son look
through the family
album: Harry Dean
Stanton (left) and Hunter
Carson (right) in *Paris,
Texas* (1984)

another is death. Lasse Hallstrom's *My Life as a Dog* (1985) centres on the growing pains of a young Swedish boy in the 1950s after the death of his mother, though it coarsens its sensibility with two gross cinematic clichés: the portrayal of Swedes as sexual obsessives; and the inadequate equating of growing up with sexual curiosity (the obligatory 'I'll show you mine if you show me yours' scene was the moment when my patience snapped with this vastly overrated movie). A much more perceptive exploration of the theme of the absent mother is to be found in Vincente Minnelli's *The Courtship of Eddie's Father* (1960), which ostensibly is about the attempt of a young boy (Ronny Howard) to marry off his widowed father (Glenn Ford), but beneath the surface is more about the complicated process by which the young Eddie comes to terms with the loss of his mother. Two scenes are justly famous: a breakfast scene where father and son seem lost in their own home and the boy, standing precariously on a footstool as he reaches for a cup and saucer, laments his inability to cry; and a later moment where the

99

sight of a dead goldfish unexpectedly rouses the boy to a paroxysm of grief. (As we shall see, child hysteria within a tense family situation will also be vividly treated in Minnelli's *Meet Me in St Louis*.)

As in *Eddie's Father*, there is also a powerful scene of displaced grief in Elia Kazan's first film, *A Tree Grows in Brooklyn* (1945), when, after failing to weep at the time of her father's death, his daughter (Peggy Ann Garner) breaks down weeks later on receiving his posthumous gift of flowers. The girl throughout has been torn in her devotion between a father (James Dunn) who is both a romantic dreamer and also an inadequate alcoholic, and a mother (Dorothy McGuire) who is a severe task-mistress but whose practicality holds the family together: beauty is truth, but so is poverty. Although future Kazan films like *East of Eden* (1954) and *Splendour in the Grass* (1961) are really about adolescent anguish and therefore outside this survey, it is worth mentioning Kazan as a director who anatomizes as well as anyone the tortured, tangled love/hate relationships between parents and children; how children are marked by them; and how if they are to survive and find their own identity, they have to grow beyond them. A graduate of the powerhouse Kazan school of directing, Sidney Lumet has treated this theme in a more overtly political context. His films, *Daniel* (1983) and

Dustin Hoffman (left) and Justin Henry (right): father and son thrown together in the family tear-jerker *Kramer vs Kramer* (1979)

100

Dreaming of a better future: father (James Dunn) and daughter (Peggy Ann Garner) in *A Tree Grows in Brooklyn* (1945)

Running on Empty (1988) ask the question: who pays for committed lives? Who pays for having passionate parents? (As we shall see, these questions are at the heart of Chris Menges's *A World Apart*.)

As a final point of fairness, however, it should perhaps be said that children themselves can bring a new dimension of difficulty into adults' lives and into a marriage. In his great autobiographical novel *Sons and Lovers* D. H. Lawrence defined the feeling very well: 'There was the halt, the wistfulness about the ensuing year which is like autumn in a man's life. His wife was casting him off and turning now for love and life to the children. Hence forward he was more or less a husk. And he half acquiesced, as so many men do, yielding their place to their children.'[1] It is that kind of situation that forces the father in *Meet Me in St Louis* to precipitate a family crisis; and the father (Fred MacMurray) in Douglas Sirk's *There's Always Tomorrow* (1956) to flirt a little with the prospect of an affair. If the effect on the father is to be marginalized and taken for granted, the corresponding effect of children on a mother might be suffocation. 'You don't know how a family can surround you at times', says the pressurized housewife in Max Ophuls's remarkable family melodrama *The Reckless Moment* (1949). Then there is the simple lesson that children will eventually become parents

101

themselves and may well duplicate the mistakes that caused them such pain. 'Your generation did screw it up', says the son (Matt Dillon) in Arthur Penn's *Target* (1985); to which his father replies cheerfully, 'Don't worry about it, yours will too.'

Meet Me in St Louis
(USA 1944: Vincente Minnelli)

'A love story between a happy family and a way of living'[2] was James Agee's description of this film, which is still one of the most popular of the great MGM musicals and an archetypal example of the MGM family film. Yet, if it also remains one of the most critically admired of musicals, the reason is perhaps the maturity with which the film explores the stresses that lie beneath the surface of this typical family, the Smiths. In this respect, the film is thematically similar to Hitchcock's extraordinary thriller of a year earlier, *Shadow of a Doubt* (1943), and coincidentally the writer of the stories on which Minnelli's film is based, Sally Benson, also wrote the excellent children's dialogue for the Hitchcock movie. Musical or not, *Meet Me in St Louis* has its moments of horror and suspense, and two particular sources of tension: the embarrassing insignificance in the family's affairs of the father (Leon Ames) who is the family's nominal head; and the neurotic personality of the family's youngest daughter, the five-year-old Tootie, played by the Sarah Bernhardt of child acting, Margaret O'Brien. The big climax will come when these two sources of tension converge.

At first, as we are lightly introduced to the family in their American Gothic house in the St Louis of 1903, father's diminishing influence is the source of some humour. It is a female-dominated household, with the mother (Mary Astor) as queen bee, and with the maid (Marjorie Main) admirably expressing the feminine bias of the household with her succinct comment about a friend of hers 'having trouble with her husband, him being a man'. Father has not even been informed that one of his daughters is expecting a proposal over their newfangled household gadget, the telephone. 'Your pappa's not supposed to know,' comments Grandpa ironically, 'it's enough that he's working hard to support you all day. . . .' When Father returns home exhausted from his day at the office, he has difficulty in laying claim to the phone and only belatedly learns of the anticipated engagement. He comments ruefully: 'Just when was I voted out of this family?' In fact, the anticipated proposal does not immediately happen. Unobtrusively, the stage is being set for a darkening of tone and also for the moment when the father will attempt to assert his authority.

Before this happens, we are also introduced to young Tootie, a morbid little moppet who carries a doll with, she says, four fatal diseases and who insists on singing 'I'll never get drunk anymore' at her sister's party. Just as we are pegging her as one of MGM's all-too-familiar precocious little monsters, Minnelli makes her up *as* a monster in the film's celebrated Hallowe'en sequence, where she is assigned to confront and insult the neighbourhood's principal bogeyman, who lives at the end of the street with his wife. The couple are interestingly characterized from Tootie's viewpoint: childless, gloomy, male-dominated, the exact antithesis of her own family. 'I hate you!' she screams at the neighbour when he answers the

Little Margaret O'Brien and Judy Garland entertain their house guests in *Meet Me in St Louis* (1944)

door, throwing flour in his face and then running down the street to rejoin her friends. 'I killed him ... I'm the most horrible', says Tootie, and it is a scene of childhood derring-do and fear of the bogeyman that was not to be equalled until the children's similar confrontation with bogeyman 'Boo' Radley in *To Kill a Mockingbird* (1962). In *Meet Me in St Louis*, it is a scene that suddenly opens up a dark door on the personality of children and their response to fearsome, authoritarian adults: it considerably modifies the idealized impression of family life given so far, and prepares for conflict to come.

It should be said that Minnelli directs this Hallowe'en sequence with considerable awareness of its potential for horror, with a sinister tracking shot down the dark street, a forceful close-up of the girl's tense face, and a shock moment when she is startled by a horse. (The reliance on atmosphere rather than visual explicitness for the terror reflects Minnelli's admiration for the subtle, poetic horror films of Val Lewton.) Significantly, Minnelli said that this sequence, 'where the children fantasize Hallowe'en as blood and thunder and get involved in all sorts of modern mischief', was one of the main reasons why he wanted to do the film. 'The burning of feet and slashing of throats they envisioned,' he went on, 'almost a wistful longing for horror, wasn't the sweet and treacly approach so characteristic of Hollywood. This was the type of fantasy that real children, raised on the grimmest of Grimms' fairy-tales, would have.'[3]

Now a real horror is ready to befall the household, when Father drops a bombshell. He is being sent to New York to better his career and proposes that the family accompany him. His determination to accept the job and uproot the family is not simply because of his better prospects and the financial rewards, but seems also an endeavour to regain respect and reclaim ascendancy in a family in which he has been shunted to the sidelines as the necessary but barely acknowledged breadwinner. At the revelation of this news, the girls at first gather round their mother and then slowly drift away from the table, leaving Father feeling, in his words, 'a criminal'.

The family will clearly survive the upheaval but as the time for their departure approaches (significantly, in winter), the mood grows increas-

Another harassed Minnelli father: Glenn Ford (right) and Ronny Howard (left) in Vincente Minnelli's *The Courtship of Eddie's Father* (1962)

ingly melancholy. In those incomparably tremulous tones of pathos, the young Judy Garland sings 'Have yourself a merry little Christmas' in a manner that reduces her sister to tears (and in the first version of the song the next line of the lyric was to be: 'It may be your last . . .'). Everything is now in place for Tootie's reaction to the move, which has gathered in her mind from a period of disruption to an impending tragedy. She rushes out into the snow towards the snow people whom she has built and attacks and beheads them, preferring them to be 'killed' rather than be left behind, and leaving the place looking more like a battlefield than a garden. In preparing Miss O'Brien (who specialized in hysteria) for this scene, Minnelli asked her mother for advice and was told that to get the required emotional responses he should simply go over and tell her that her dog was to be kidnapped and killed. The resulting scene has an intensity that, as Agee suggested, demonstrated Miss O'Brien's dramatic readiness for the role of the tormented child in Ibsen's *The Wild Duck*. We have travelled a long way from happy families and the usual Utopia of the MGM musical.

Having witnessed this scene, in which he has been symbolically decapitated by his own daughter, what must Father do? He summons the family downstairs and tells them he has decided they will stay in St Louis after all. It is not simply a change of mind, or even heart: it is as if an evil spell has been lifted. 'In a very complicated camera movement,' says the critic Thomas Elsaesser, describing the moment very well, 'Minnelli conveys the precise feeling of a rhythm recommencing' and the characters circulate once more through the house 'as if their blood had begun to flow again'.[4] Father has restored harmony to the household, but the hidden sacrifice is his own satisfaction: more that that, manhood.

BICYCLE THIEVES

(Italy 1948 : Vittorio de Sica)

Either as mute witnesses or vulnerable victims of the war and post-war environment created by their elders, children play an important role in the films of Italian neo-realism. Their return to the city at the end of Roberto Rossellini's *Rome — Open City* (1945) signifies a hope for the future, whereas the suicide of the young Berlin boy at the end of Rossellini's *Germany — Year Zero* (1948) stands for a childhood that has been destroyed just as surely as the city around him. Also memorable are the child-observer of de Sica's *The Children are Watching Us* (1944) and the criminal children of the same director's *Shoeshine* (1946): essentially witnesses or victims of adult corruption or failure. Yet perhaps no neo-realist child is as memorable as Bruno (Enzio Staiola), the wide-eyed chubby-cheeked boy who accompanies his father Antonio Ricci (Lamberto Maggiorani) one hot Sunday on a search for the man's stolen bicycle that is the means to his livelihood. In plot terms, Bruno is irrelevant to *Bicycle Thieves:* in emotional and ethical terms, he is indispensable to it.

Bruno is first seen polishing his father's bicycle in readiness for the latter's first day at his new job: this gesture somehow seems an amplification of his father's rediscovered joy and pride. With hindsight the only disturbing note is Bruno's discovery of a blemish on the bike he has not noticed before, a foretaste of his enforced recognition of the blemishes in his father's character that are to be revealed when his bicycle is stolen and the pressure of his situation intensifies. Another discomforting detail in the opening section is a moment when the father is being taught how to paste up posters in his new job (pointedly, it is a poster for Rita Hayworth in *Gilda*, the ultimate glamorous contrast to neo-realist grittiness) and he and his helpmate are pestered by two boys begging for money. When they are brusquely dismissed, we see them as they follow another man and are also pushed aside. It is an unemphatic background detail of milieu that nevertheless offers a quick sketch of post-war impoverishment and a suggestion that certain social situations and failures are putting children at risk.

A different kind of risk is indicated in a later scene when father, son and some friends have gone to the market to search for the missing bicycle. Bruno is assigned to inspect bells and pumps to see if he recognizes them and, as he does so, he is approached by an older man who clearly wants to pick him up. It is another disturbing sketch of the vulnerablility of children in this kind of society, and an implicit indictment of the father who, in his growing obsession with his own problems, will forget his son. Bruno slips and falls without his father noticing and is not even allowed to urinate before his father is hustling him on. At this stage the dangers or discomforts tend to be physical. Later Bruno must confront the disillusionment of his father's spiritual world.

At one moment, sheltering from the rain, Bruno finds himself amongst a group of clergymen who are babbling at each other in German. It is a disquieting experience for him, one feels, both because German must still have seemed a menacing language in Italy at that time and because the incident seems a metaphor for Bruno's situation: a child in a grown-up dilemma who feels as though he is lost in a country where he does not speak the language. Later, in looking for an old man in a church who can help them in their enquiries, Bruno inadvertently disturbs a priest in his confessional and is crisply clipped across the head for his pains: so much for churchly compassion. This blow is followed by a more serious incident when his father strikes him for seeming to criticize him (and thus symbolically challenging his manhood). It is a sign of the father's increasing disintegration and desperation.

Momentarily separated after their argument, father and son are reunited after the former has been caught up in a crowd surrounding an accident on a beach and has momentarily feared that Bruno might have been drowned. It is the one incident in the film that smacks of some contrivance, yet it is also the one moment in the film when the father is brought to look at the loss of his bicycle in a larger perspective. It is, after all, a small thing compared to the loss of a son, and suggests Bruno, in structural terms, as an important counterpoint to the bicycle. As a token of contrition, the father takes Bruno to a restaurant for a meal they can barely afford and in their anxiety can hardly eat, but which, as André Bazin says, is a scene that represents 'an oasis' in the film – a temporary flight from poverty, a sharing in the kind of life others so thoughtlessly enjoy. Bruno occasionally looks over to a banquet at a lavishly-set table opposite, and is eyed condescendingly by an

The sympathetic son and the defeated father at a low point in *Bicycle Thieves* (1948)

astutely cast, extraordinary-looking boy who, in his appearance (he looks rather like Martin Stephens in *The Innocents*), projects an air of pampered pomposity and precociousness. He is a remarkable miniature of mockery and of a society with a sneering insensitivity to the deprived and unfortunate.

Eventually the father will track down the thief and Bruno will obligingly bring a policeman, but there is no proof or witness to support Ricci's case: like Henry Fonda in Hitchcock's *The Wrong Man* (1957), he has all the indignation of the wronged but the evidence contrives to slide tantalizingly through his fingers. (By a curious coincidence, there is a strong physical resemblance between the actor who plays the father/victim in de Sica's film and the man who will play the villain in Hitchcock's.) After the accused has had an epileptic fit, father and son must back away from an angry crowd. They slump on a kerb directly opposite a football stadium, where the mass of parked bicycles outside the ground suddenly assumes the proportions of a nightmarish extension of Ricci's despair. As he prepares to steal a bicycle himself, he tells Bruno to go away and catch the tram home. He can only commit the act away from his son's gaze. Bruno has been his companion, his shadow. Now he is the conscience that Ricci must shut out.

In fact, the theft goes wrong and Ricci is caught, and almost beaten up and sent to the police, However, seeing Bruno's anguish and sensing Ricci's dejected defeatism, the owner of the bicycle decides to let the thief go, with the admonition: 'What an example to your son . . .' The father cannot look at Bruno but the boy, who has been constantly looking up at (implicitly, *to*) his father, now takes his hand in a gesture of sympathy and equality, the bond of their love the only certainty in the dark, hostile and uncertain world into which they disappear.

Critics of neo-realist cinema tend to focus their reservations on three particular areas: its lack of a political analysis of society that would expose the reasons for poverty rather than simply survey its effects; its over-emphasis on external reality at the expense of the characters' inner lives; and its use of children as emotional blackmail. Bruno in *Bicycle Thieves* is an interesting figure to consider in relation to these arguments. He is not simply there for the purposes of 'emotional blackmail': the child's-eye view is crucial to an understanding of and empathy with Ricci's loss of dignity, for it is Bruno's admiration of his father that gives the ending its impact – the father could endure public humiliation but his tears are for the fact that his son has witnessed it. Moreover, Bruno supplies the key to the inner life of Ricci, which critics say neo-realism too often ignores: he is the father's conscience, compassion and finally his companion and confidante, walking not behind him as before but *beside* him. As for the absence of political analysis, de Sica always claimed his neo-realism was social, not communist, and if he dealt with the problems of the poor, it was out of love of mankind. Bruno is an important vessel of that love, the means by which an audience's moral sympathies can be engaged and possibly enlarged. This is not to deny other aspects of the film that contribute to its impact, notably a screenplay by Cesare Zavattini that charts an obsession with an invincible purity of line and an absolute simplicity of means. But it is Bruno who gives the film its great heart.

THE MISCHIEF-MAKERS – LES MISTONS
(France 1957: François Truffaut)

A beautiful teenage girl, Bernardette (Bernardette Lafont), is seen cycling on a sunny day, the travelling shot giving a vividly immediate sense of release and youthful vitality. She is watched by a gang of young boys, who see in her a dream-princess of overpowering beauty. They follow her into the woods and prowl around her bike. In a shot of restrained slow motion, one of them sniffs the saddle, as if trying to inhale something of its rider's presence and sensuality. 'Innocent hearts have their own childish logic', says the narrator over the soundtrack (the film is based on a short story, 'Virginales', by Maurice Pons). 'Too young to love, they decide to hate her.'

Their hatred takes the form of disrupting her romance with her boyfriend, a gym teacher called Gerard (Gerard Blain). They startle the lovers in a deserted stadium; watch them with mocking envy on a tennis court; jeer when the two kiss in a cinema. What started as a game becomes a kind of military campagn in which 'the enemy' must be humiliated. When the lovers are separated, they send a postcard to Bernardette signed 'Les Mistons' and rudely suggestive about what she will get up to when reunited with Gerard. However, there is to be no reunion. Gerard is killed in a mountaineering accident. When they see Bernardette for a final time, it is in complete contrast to the opening shot. She is now on foot and wearing a dark sombre dress, as if her own youthful innocence has now been cloaked by a darkening recognition of mortality. Recalling the whole episode the narrator's final comment is to say that his recollection is one of compassion rather than shame.

This early Truffaut short is about a summer interlude, possibly influenced by the Bergman film of that name or by Bergman's *Summer with Monika* (1952) and certainly seeming an influence on Robert Mulligan's similarly structured film of first love and lost innocence, *Summer of '42* (1971). Its gradual darkening of tone following an exhilarating opening will be the structural pattern of a number of future Truffaut movies, particularly his masterpiece, *Jules et Jim* (1961), which it also anticipates with its nature imagery, its cycling motif, its use of narration, and its close observation of love abruptly ended by death.

'Most films about children make the adults serious and the child frivolous', said Truffaut in an interview in *The New Yorker* (20 February 1960). 'Quite the other way round.' Indeed, for all the humour, summertime imagery, self-consciously poetic narrative and Gallic romance, the tone of *Les Mistons* is surprisingly cruel. There is no trace of sentimentality about the children. We are never allowed to get close to them: appropriately enough, for the cruelty stems from their roles as observers on the outside of adult experience. Because they have as yet no point of entry to adulthood and so their greed for experience is frustrated, their fascination takes the form of alternately studied and sadistic contempt.

I can think of few films that show the world of childhood and adulthood as being so thoroughly antagonistic, or see a larger gulf between the two states: the young adults either heedless or intolerant towards the children, the 'mistons' either derisory or demonic towards their elders. Unlike Carson McCullers's enstranged Frankie Adams, these mischief-makers are not yearning to be members of the wedding: they would rather cause havoc at the engagement.

DAYS OF HEAVEN
(USA 1978: Terrence Malick)

Texas, 1916. Two drifters, Abby (Brooke Adams) and Bill (Richard Gere), who are posing as sister and brother but who are actually lovers, come to work on a rich man's farm. The farmer (Sam Shepard) falls in love with Abby and proposes marriage. Having heard the farmer's doctor intimating that the farmer has at best a year to live, Bill suggests to Abby that she should accept: the inheritance will at last give them some security. However, the marriage seems to rejuvenate the farmer and, what is more, Abby seems to be genuinely falling in love with him. Yet two calamities are in store. The farmer sees 'brother and sister' kissing, and his suspicions about their relationship will lead to murderous conflagration. Also Abby's parasitical marriage seems to precipitate a Hardyesque convulsion of Nature, for a plague of locusts swoops on to the farm.

Such a summary might imply that *Days of Heaven* is a very melodramatic film and stuffed with narrative incident. Few audiences, however, will have experienced the film like that. There are three particular elements that ensure that the events are kept at an objective arm's length: Malick's oblique and ironic direction, which favours natural detail over narrative drive; Nestor Almendros's photography, whose golden sheen over these days of heaven is so visually splendid as to dwarf the psychology of the characters; and, perhaps most of all, the film's detached point of view, which is substantially that of Bill's younger sister, Linda (Linda Manz). As he did in his first film, *Badlands* (1974), Malick uses the device of a young female narrator to comment on the events of the narrative. It casts a shadow of innocence over far from innocent events and exploits, for purposes of irony, richness and ambiguity, the gap we perceive between the narrator's perception of events and our own.

Malick has said that the model for Linda's commentary was Henry James's *What Maisie Knew*, a novel that explores adult hypocrisy and cruelty about sex and love through the eyes of a young girl, who may or may not have understood and been subtly corrupted by what she has seen. 'It was to be the fate of this patient little girl,' says James in his opening chapter, 'to see much more than she at first understood, but also even at first to understand much more than any little girl, however patient, perhaps ever understood before.' The conception of seeing 'more than she at first understood' seems to lie at the heart of *Days of Heaven*.

For all its massive visual qualities, *Days of Heaven* has a peculiarly literary flavour, partly because of its understatement and density, but also because of its narration (a device that very often gives off that kind of literary aroma, as in Kubrick's *Barry Lyndon*, (1975), or in the use of voice-over in numerous recent film adaptations of period English novels). As well as its Jamesian associations, the film has evocations of Twain's *The Adventures of Huckleberry Finn*, when the trio are escaping along the river after the accidental death of the farmer, and also when the ending has the girl and her friend escaping from institutionalized life and 'civilization' and

110

The child/narrator/observer of *Days of Heaven*: Linda Manz (1978)

'lighting out for the territory', as it were. The narration also draws attention to elements that are part of the story but are not given especial visual prominence – for example, Linda's acquisition of knowledge and a little education from the farmer. ('He taught me about keys on the piano . . . notes . . . he taught me about parts of the globe.') However, the most striking paradox is that the very simplicity of the narration makes the film more, not less, mysterious, because what we are seeing is not what she is telling and the conclusions she draws are sometimes not ours. Is this evidence of her childlike naïveté, or an instinctive wisdom that we have since lost?

Because they are viewed through a child's eyes the adults do become stranger, a little larger-than-life and, in the idyllic passage after the marriage in the middle of the film, like gods and goddesses out of a fairy-tale. This might explain the sumptuous photography and the film's title; and again it is something that is very like Henry James's conception in *What Maisie Knew*, where young Maisie treads through experience like an enchanted child in a menacing forest. One significant difference between Malick and James here is that, whereas James's vocabulary often seems too sophisticated for a child, Linda's vocabulary in *Days of Heaven* seems not sophisticated enough for the complexity of experience. She records, but does not explain – for

111

example, why Abby and Bill pretend to be brother and sister, or why the farmer falls in love with Abby ('maybe it was the way the wind blew through her hair'). In her restrained way, she romanticizes, but sometimes quite wrongly. 'There was nobody by his side', she says about the farmer, when, in fact, the paternal devotion to him of his foreman (the performance of his career by that grizzled Hollywood heavy Robert Wilke) will be the main driving force behind the hunting down and killing of her brother. Similarly, after the farmer's death, Linda says of Abby that 'She blamed it on herself. She didn't care if she was happy or not. She just wanted to make up for what she had done.' This might be a discreet suggestion of Linda's moral sense (as James subtly hints at Maisie's moral judgements on what is going on around her), but this view of Abby is not reinforced by any visual evidence. Indeed, the impression we get is that she comes through the double tragedy relatively unscathed and more than capable of looking after herself.

Malick's skilful use, then, of Linda's limitations and yet individuality as a narrator makes for a fascinating counterpoint between the story told visually (and it often seems like a silent film) and the verbal commentary. This counterpoint serves to emphasize the unknowability of human motive but also the fascinating and unique way a child assimilates and evaluates experience. For Linda, it is a story of adventure, and a hesitant evolution of her social philosophy, but her matter-of-factness keeps a sense of wonder under control. When she and the three adults are living a life of luxury, their splendid isolation is drily and prosaically rendered: 'I tell you the rich have got it figured out ... Nobody sent us a letter. We didn't receive no cards ...'

During this period, their only visitors are a flying circus, who put on a screening of Chaplin's classic short *The Immigrant* (1916), showing its most famous and remarkable moment – when the immigrants, all sentimentally watching the Statue of Liberty as they sail past on their entry into America, are suddenly roped together like cattle by the immigration authorities. (As we shall see, Louis Malle's *Au Revoir, les Enfants* will quote this same sequence, to different effect, but with similarly devastating results.) The Chaplin reference is relevant to *Days of Heaven*, with its similar sympathy for the hobo and outsider, and its similar ambivalence towards America as New World, as land of opportunity. Indeed, it is possible to take the Chaplin analogy further and see *Days of Heaven* as a version and variation of Chaplin's *The Kid* as seen from the kid's point of view: similarly threatened with separation and institutionalization and similarly rescued by a friend. Even Linda's comment, 'You just got half-devil, half-angel in you ...' causes a fleeting remembrance of Chaplin's evocation of Dreamland in *The Kid*.

Linda has two moments of prophecy in the film. Early on, she tells of a meeting with a man who talks to her of hell-fire and apocalypse: 'He told me the whole earth was going up in flames ... There's gonna be creatures running every which way, some of them burned, half their wings burning. People are gonna be screamin' and hollerin' for help.' It is an anticipation of the locust plague and the fire, which, in some way, Abby and Bill seem to have brought with them (if Abby is a parasite, Bill is first seen stoking a furnace). During their escape on the river, Linda also has a terrifying vision:

'Some sights that I saw was really spooky that it gave me goose pimples and that I felt like cold hands touchin' the back of my neck and . . . it could be the dead comin' for me or somethin'.' This death-saturated child's vision – evocative of Hardy's doomed child, little Father Time in *Jude the Obscure* – seems not only a premonition of her brother's fate but also an omen of universal destruction to come: as the film closes, men are preparing to march off to the suicidal battlefields of the First World War. Overall, *Days of Heaven* has a remarkable vision to offer: of Heaven and Hell, angels and devils, a lost Eden and emergent America, all calmly appraised by a resilient, post-industrial kid launching herself at the twentieth century.

A WORLD APART

(GB 1988: Chris Menges)

In Sir Richard Attenborough's anti-apartheid movie, *Cry Freedom* (1987), the major dramatic event after the death of Steve Biko is the scene when the young daughter of the newspaper editor, Donald Woods, who has befriended Biko and is now under house arrest, receives a T-shirt through the post which has been intercepted by the Security Police and saturated with acid-based powder. It is a crucial turning-point in the action. Woods's wife now revises her objections to her husband's political stand and says that he must go ahead with his book that exposes the truth, and he also decides that he must take his family out of the country. It is an incident that also shocks some of his less politically active friends. The true nature of a political system, the film seems to be saying, can be determined by its behaviour towards children. In this regard, the film's flashback finale – the massacre at Soweto in 1976 where hundreds of black children were killed by the security forces – is structurally peculiar but thematically essential.

The effect of apartheid on the child is also the main theme of Chris Menges's *A World Apart*, but seen in more comprehensive and complex terms. The child in this case is a 13-year-old girl, Molly Roth (Jodhi May), whose problems come, like Woods's daughter, not directly from apartheid but from being the daughter of politically active parents who oppose it. Her father, who has to go underground when the African National Congress, which he supports, is outlawed, appears only in the opening scene and is not seen again. Her mother, Diana (Barbara Hershey) is a journalist whose continuing support for the blacks in South Africa brings her into conflict with the authorities.

The impact of her parents' political commitment has a deeply disorientating effect on Molly. It provokes alienation and hostility amongst her colleagues at school, who taunt her with jibes about her 'unpatriotic' parents. This builds to a painful scene when she is refused entrance to her friend's house and is roughly dragged home by her friend's father, who disapproves strongly of her parents' attitudes. Yet she is not only becoming an outsider in the world of her immediate schoolfriends, but also an outsider in her parents' world, for she is not taken into their confidence. As Menges discreetly shows in visual terms, there are rooms she had better not enter, drawers she had better not open, windows from which she can only observe. The *natural* alienation implicit in certain stories of childhood is felt in an extreme degree in Molly. Her bewilderment is emphasized by her role

Mother and daughter in
the fight against
apartheid: Barbara
Hershey (left) and Jodhi
May (right) in *A World
Apart* (1988)

as observer in paired sequences that have conflicting implications – for
example, two party scenes, one polite, posh and for whites only, the other
more informal, for blacks, that is raided by the police; or two history
lessons, one from the perspective of an Afrikaner, another by a black man,
which give a completely different account of the evolution of their nation.
Molly is seen attending two church services, one at her (white) school
assembly, the other at the church of her (black) maid. It is noticeable that in
neither service does she join in with the singing: she clearly does not know
where she belongs, whose voices she can join. Only at the end, during the
funeral of her maid's brother, Solomon, who has died in police custody, can
she join with her mother in the African hymn and at last feel and express
solidarity with her and the movement she supports.

Molly's emotional turmoil has undoubtedly been exacerbated by her
relationship with her mother, and her feeling of rejection and isolation
because of her mother's intense preoccupation with politics. She feels she is
not loved, or loved less than she ought to be because of her mother's work.
This comes to a head when Diana is arrested under the new 90-day detention
act, and then re-arrested for a further 90 days when the first period comes to
an end (and it is a measure of Menges' secure pacing of the film that this
period of detention is made to feel an appreciably long time). Molly has to be

114

looked after by her grandmother, with whom she does not get on. Diana is finally released but there is a further blow for Molly: the discovery of a suicide note written by her mother in a period of depression in prison. Diana explains she was afraid she was to be tortured and might betray her friends, but for Molly it is shattering evidence that politics seem more important to Diana than her family or her daughter. It takes the news of Solomon's murder and the subsequent funeral to bring Molly to a new understanding of her mother's beliefs and priorities.

At this point it perhaps should be stressed that *A World Apart*, like *Cry Freedom*, is based on a true story. 'Diana' is really Ruth First, who was to be assassinated by letter-bomb in Maputo, Mozambique, in 1982, and her daughter 'Molly' is in reality the film's screenwriter, Shawn Slovo, who seems to have written the script as a kind of exorcism. Débutant director Chris Menges, who is perhaps better known as the Oscar-winning cameraman of *The Killing Fields* (1984) and *The Mission* (1986), adds his own touch of authentic recollection, for one of his first jobs as a cameraman was on a programme on South Africa for Independent Television's *World in Action* series at the time the events recorded by the film were unfolding. It was a formative influence on his career as a film-maker, he says. Like *Cry Freedom*, *A World Apart* casts English actors as South African policemen as an implicit condemnation of the British Government's inaction against apartheid, and, also like Attenborough's film, therefore had the distinction (the honour, it would say) of being pointedly boycotted by Government representatives. Nevertheless, also like *Cry Freedom*, it is essentially an attack on apartheid from the viewpoint of a liberal humanitarian white man, with international stars in order to attract an international audience; and it runs into the kinds of contradictions and compromises that involves.

In *Cry Freedom*, necessary though it might have been to get the message across to as large an audience as possible, the compromise came from elevating as hero the white newspaperman Donald Woods (Kevin Kline) over the black political activist Steve Biko (Denzel Washington). In *A World Apart*, the compromise (perhaps, in this case, imbalance might be a better word) comes from the way the mother/daughter relationship seems to complicate and even diminish the political message. In an interview in *The Guardian* (August 1988) Menges talked about the films in terms of 'the mother caught up in the conflict between work and family' and added that 'you could also say it is in a sense about a lost childhood'. Certainly one of the interesting and original features of *A World Apart* is that its main protagonist is a woman. The policemen comment on how lucky she is that South Africans respect their womenfolk – the implication being that otherwise she would have been tortured – but that respect is clearly beginning to wear thin as she carries on refusing to help them, putting her at greater physical risk. The other argument put to her though, by the most sympathetic of her interrogators (David Suchet), is that this kind of political activity is something that a woman should not do and that, as a consequence, Diana has been 'a terrible mother'.

The film does not endorse this as a judgement on Diana's character, but certainly one effect of filtering the experience through the child's eyes is to shift the political drama on to a more domestic level. Like the children in a

number of Sidney Lumet's dramas, notably *Daniel* (1983), Molly is a victim of having committed parents. Politics generally (not just the South African political system specifically) are seen as something alienating and obstructive that can undermine the family. There is nothing untruthful about this, but it somewhat compromises the anti-apartheid thrust of the film, which becomes more a domestic melodrama on the theme of the neglected child. It takes a film like *Mapantsula* (1988) to give an insider's view of apartheid on film. For all their confusions, *Cry Freedom* and *A World Apart* can be applauded for the decency and humanity of their attitudes, and for their poignant observations on the contribution of blind adult prejudice to the suffering of children.

Another child victim of colonialist brutality: the policeman (Bob Peck) tortures the servant boy (Edwin Mahinda) to obtain information in Harry Hook's *The Kitchen Toto* (1987)

CHAPTER SIX

BRAT PACKS

As a kid he probably wanted to be a suspect when he grew up.

(Peter Yates's *The Janitor*)

What chance have they got in a place like this? They call them enemies of society . . . why not?

(William Wyler's *Dead End*)

MOST films about childhood situate children in relation to their parents or some form of adult society. Not many consider the private society children create for themselves. This chapter concerns the cinematic representation of the gang, and the way it has evolved from the exuberant anarchy of the Dead End Kids, whose energy can be channelled into more constructive areas, to the neurotic nihilism of the youngsters in *River's Edge*, who seem totally without moral bearings.

In cinematic terms, the gang is sometimes presented as a kind of alternative society, with its own rules and rituals, and with a wary scepticism of the class-based, adult-regulated, mainstream. *Hue and Cry* and *Stand By Me* are good examples of that.

Another filmic convention is to see the gang as a social problem, where youths are polarized into tribal opposition based on race (as in *West Side Story*) or class (*Quadrophenia*) or territory (*Rumble Fish*); or where they direct their hostilities at a world whose values they fundamentally despise, as in *Los Olvidados*. A movie like *Bad News Bears* offers a quirkily comic variation on the theme, uniting a disparate gang of tearaways, under the banner of a baseball team. This gives the team the common purpose and group solidarity of the gang, and also extends the theme into a more general disquisition on the possibilities of social cohesion and even democracy.

117

Another idiosyncrasy of the film is the incorporation of a girl into the structure. In film, the gang has been almost exclusively a male preserve. *Girls Town* has yet to be made.

Rainbow Harvest (left) and Sarah Boyd (right) play girls from very different backgrounds who strike up a summer friendship in Marissa Silver's *Old Enough* (1984).

DEAD END
(USA 1937: William Wyler)
ANGELS WITH DIRTY FACES
(USA 1938: Michael Curtiz)

'A weird band of commercial adolescents'[1] was critic David Thomson's description of the Dead End Kids (Bobby Jordan, Huntz Hall, Billy Halop, Leo Gorcey, Bernard Punsley and Gabriel Dell), who were later to become the more respectably entitled Bowery Boys. They shot to fame in two gangster film classics of the 1930s, *Dead End* and *Angels with Dirty Faces*, which show significant contrasts in their attitudes to the responsibility of the individual and society for childhood criminality.

Adapted by Lillian Hellman from the play by Sidney Kingsley, *Dead End* opens in a way that, nearly a quarter of a century later, would be aped by the film version of *West Side Story* (1961) – a panoramic view of New York that closes in on one particular environment, in this case a street on New York's East Side where the tenement dwellings of the poor adjoin the opulent apartments of the wealthy. Indeed, *Dead End* might well have been a big influence on the film of *West Side Story*, particularly in its stylistic mix of realism and theatricality.

During the filming director Willian Wyler was sacked for a day by his producer, Sam Goldwyn, because Goldwyn claimed the set of the slum looked dirty (Lillian Hellman came out in sympathy). Wyler would have preferred filming on location, for although Richard Day's set is one of the film's most striking features – a labyrinthine trap that confirms the divisions between rich and poor and the difficulty of escaping from or rising above one's surroundings – it does look excessively artificial in the context of the film's social observations and analysis. This in turn gives a somewhat theatrical flavour to the film's argument, which is basically a plea for liberal reform in the era of Roosevelt's New Deal and a straightforward declaration of poverty as the root cause of crime.

The Dead End Kids, who are the undisciplined offspring of this environment, direct their hostilities particularly against the rich boy who lives in the luxury apartment opposite. When they beat him up and the boy's father comes to his aid, one of the Dead End Kids, Tommy (Billy Halop), stabs the older man and has to go on the run. What unites the Dead End Kids and the other poor people in their area, notably a struggling architect, Dave (Joel McCrae), and Tommy's sister, Drina (Sylvia Sidney), is a suspicion of the police as agents of repression. What will divide them, however, are their respective attitudes to a gangster, Baby-Face Martin (Humphrey Bogart), who has been brought up in these slums, but who has got out and is now making a sentimental return to see his mother (Marjorie Main) and his former girlfriend, Francey (Claire Trevor). As an architect, Dave wants to pull down the slums and build a better place that would rid us of the Martins of this world. As an elder sister, Drina wants to prevent her brother Tommy from going the way of Martin. But for the Dead End Kids Martin is a hero. More than that, as Graham Greene has shrewdly noted, he is their adult guide to the future – 'They carry his baton in their pockets. He was brought up in the same dead end and like a friendly Old Boy he gives them tips – how to catch another gang unawares, how to fling a knife.'[2]

119

'See this shirt?' says Martin to the boys, 'Silk, 20 bucks. See this suit? Custom tailored, 150 bucks.' Like all classic gangster heroes, Martin preens himself on his appearance, which becomes a badge of his heightened status. Yet, as his reunions with mother (who violently rejects him) and sweetheart (who has become a streetwalker) turn into encounters with disillusionment, Martin will become an increasingly tragic figure who has not really escaped the trappings of his upbringing at all, his 'baby face' a melancholy reminder of his remaining a Dead End Kid at heart. A confrontation with the architect will eventually lead to Martin's death. The reward money for Martin will be used by Dave to procure a good lawyer for Drina's brother Tommy, so that he can get a better start in life and not wind up like Martin, perishing in the slums from which he started.

In his incisive autobiographical recollections of his film-going experience, *The Devil Finds Work*, James Baldwin exposed some of the false notes of *Dead End*: its pious architect, Dave, its prim and pitying shopgirl, Drina, but as for 'the gangster, his broken mother and his broken girl – yes, I had seen *that*'.[3] Although the film's analysis is simplified and Utopian and its characterization romanticized, it did bring a new dimension of sociology into the gangster film; did offer an incisive dissection of class envy in American society (no one in American film has ever surpassed Wyler as a director of this theme); and did bring an unusual authenticity to the complex codes and rituals of the childhood gang. It did also articulate some of the anguish and anxiety of the poor that, if unrelieved or neglected or ignored, must inevitably rub off on the next generation. 'What chance have they got in a place like this?' cries Dave at one stage. 'They call them enemies of society . . . *why not*?'

Superficially, *Angels with Dirty Faces* might seem very similar to *Dead End*. Rocky Sullivan (James Cagney) is this film's equivalent of Baby-Face Martin, a gangster who returns to his old neighbourhood and quickly becomes a hero to the Dead End Kids. Through the character of Rocky, the film expresses some of the social anger that animated *Dead End*: 'They hounded us when we were hungry and wanted to eat, they hounded us when didn't want to live in those dumps they call houses, they hounded us when we found we couldn't get the fine things all around us and took 'em for ourselves.' As James Baldwin recognized from his own experience a basic truth in the character of Baby-Face Martin, so James Cagney recognized an authenticity about Rocky Sullivan. He enhanced this by drawing on a memory from his own childhood of a pimp he had observed on First Avenue who had the habit of hitching up his trousers, twisting his neck and giving out the greeting, 'Whadda you hear? Whadda you say?' However, in several important respects, *Angels* differs from *Dead End*. Whereas Wyler's film offers reform as the answer to crime, *Angel* offers religion. Whereas Wyler's film blames society for delinquency, Curtiz's film puts it down to individual choice.

The difference is particularly made clear through Rocky's friendship with Father Connolly (Pat O'Brien). In their youth they had both been tearaways on the East Side, but when they had been spotted breaking into a boxcar young Connolly could run fast enough to escape, whereas the young Rocky was caught, thus beginning the procession of reformatory and prison,

James Cagney teaches the Dead End Kids to play ball in *Angels With Dirty Faces* (1938): Leo Gorcey (in the vest) and Billy Halop are on his right; Bernard Punsley is on his left, and, behind Punsley, Gabriel Dell

which, the film implies, far from rehabilitating him, merely honed his criminal instincts. However, the failure of the prison system as a deterrent is given less emphasis than the fact that here are two boys from the same background, one of whom has become a hoodlum, the other a priest. There are two moral implications the film invites us to draw from this. The first is that in a situation or society that is oppressive and unjust, the individual can choose either to react against it violently from the outside or seek humanely to reform it from within. The second is that social conditions in themselves do not produce criminals for, after all, Rocky and Connolly are both from the same background but have chosen very different ways. Again it comes down to the individual.

However, when it comes to evaluating the message, there is the problem of charisma. This had been part of the background ambiguity, or confusion, of *Dead End*, where the sombre architect seemed so much less desirable a role-model to just about every lively youngster than the attractive Baby-

Face Martin. In *Angels with Dirty Faces*, this crucial contrast is even more marked. 'What's the use of preaching honesty,' wails Father Connolly, 'when all around you you can see dishonesty winning out?' It seems more than that. Because of Cagney's performance, Rocky Sullivan seems to offer a dynamic alternative to conventional social forms of the priest's dully conceived recreation centre. He is not simply the inevitable future for dead end kids, but an *attractive* future.

The crux of the argument is reached in the film's famous finale. Father Connolly has been waging a campaign against the racketeers, which has brought him into conflict with Rocky's shady business partner, the crooked lawyer Frazier (Humphrey Bogart) and an equally crooked politician, Keefer (George Bancroft), who want Connolly killed. Instead Rocky kills them but is sentenced to the electric chair. In his death cell, Rocky is visited by Father Connolly who pleads with him not to die a hero, otherwise the kids will admire him and possibly wind up in the same predicament. 'You're asking me to give up the only thing I have left', says Rocky, meaning dignity in death, and refuses. However, on the way to the chair he begins to whimper and grow hysterical, and the next day the shocked boys read in the paper that their hero died a coward. 'It's true, boys, every word of it', says Father Connolly, and asks them to join him in saying a prayer for 'a boy who couldn't run as fast as I could'.

This ending is a masterpiece of skilled ambiguity in that it allows everyone to have it both ways. Rocky revels in gangsterdom but is then shown up as a coward; or Rocky redeems himself at the last by feigning cowardice in order to save the souls of his Dead End disciples. He also finally puts friendship above pride (indeed it is friendship that has got him into this situation), which makes the priest's behaviour by contrast seem both devious and dubious: in a way Father Connolly betrays the memory and self-image of his friend. (The socially respectable, treacherous friend, who will bring Cagney to justice, is to be a similarly ambiguous figure in the 1949 Cagney classic *White Heat*, and played by another O'Brien, Edmond.) It is also arguable whether shattering the kid's hero-worship and illusions and leading them into the church is offering them anything other than a temporary solution. Nevertheless, ambiguous or not, the strategy of *Angels with Dirty Faces* is revealed to be fundamentally different in kind from *Dead End*. It is not social change that will rescue these kids from the streets: it is shining individual example.

HUE AND CRY
(GB 1947: Charles Crichton)

The first really successful Ealing comedy, *Hue and Cry*, makes an interesting contrast to the American films discussed above. Here the boys are not antagonistic to the police but do their work for them, bringing to justice a gang of crooks who have been plotting their crimes with the aid of a children's comic *The Trump*, which they have used as a means of passing coded information.

In his autobiography, *This is Where I Came In*, the screenwriter T. E. B. Clarke has said that the producer Henry Cornelius 'had in mind a picture based on what might be called the freemasonry among boys, all of them participants in that life of semi-fantasy exclusive to boyhood which can be so satisfying in the brief time it lasts'.[4] The aim was to create a situation that only boys could handle and build to a finale (which was conceived first) in which, for an hour, London becomes, in a sense, the boys' town and they take over the city. The film was premièred in London during the fuel shortage of 1947 and Clarke, Cornelius and director Charles Crichton feared the worst when a grim-faced Press settled down for their press-show in their overcoats. However, the critics were delighted with the film and their enthusiasm was shared by the public.

Some of its appeal was undoubtedly due to Clarke's typically eccentric and ingenious plotting, which was to reach its peak five years later in *The Lavender Hill Mob*. (This has my favourite child's line in movies: the girl in the school refusing to give up her gold Eiffel Tower miniature despite being offered an identical model in exchange by an exasperated Alec Guinness and Stanley Holloway, and when asked to say what on earth difference there is between them, retorts: 'This one's *mine*'.) However, its main appeal was probably its tone of mild anarchy and fantasy, which came as stark relief in a post-war period of stringent rationing and regulations. Some of the film was shot on a bombed building-site near St Paul's Cathedral, and although the eminent Ealing film historian Charles Barr has poured scorn on those critics who have labelled the film 'neo-realist' in consequence, there *is* an atmosphere to the film that does remind one of post-war Italian film: as in a neo-realist film like de Sica's *Shoeshine*, the stars of *Hue and Cry* are the children and the setting. It is an example of the impact and influence of documentary film on British cinema, but, unusually, the realist settings are used as a background for comedy. In this, it anticipates Billy Wilder's use of a bombed-out, post-war Berlin as an authentic setting for his black comedy about black-marketeering, *A Foreign Affair* (1948).

Writing in 1976 about *Hue and Cry*, Charles Barr might not have been impressed by its realist credentials but, writing in 1947, the critics undoubtedly were: nearly all of them referred to it as a crucial part of the film's impact. The energy and games displayed on this devastated setting not only animated the landscape, but also seemed to herald a new post-war generation emerging unscathed from the ravages of war. (A later Ealing film, Alexander Mackendrick's *Mandy*, would, as we have seen, use a similar setting to make a much less affirmative, more complex statement.) Also the setting provided a counterpoint to the action, as one boy's daydream, dismissed by his adult superiors, swells into full-blown adventure. This is one Ealing film that vindicates imagination.

Sometimes fantasy is cut down to size by mundane reality, like the moment when an imaginative reverie by young Harry Fowler is interrupted by his mother with the words, 'You've got sausage on your chin'. 'I don't think you're really a bad boy,' says a policeman to the lad, 'just a bit imaginative': it is a common refrain among the elders. 'Don't daydream in my time', the boy is told by his boss (Jack Warner), who will turn out to be the chief crook: the boy's daydreaming will lead to his 'doing time'. The heightened suspense that precedes the boy's meeting with the writer of the comic stories – ominous staircase shots, the shadow of a black cat on the wall – is deliciously punctured by the appearance of the writer himself, Alastair

Sim at his most delightfully dotty, murmuring 'O how I loathe adventurous-minded boys'. Nevertheless, suspense and realism do come together in the savage struggle between Warner and Fowler: a fight amidst those crumbling buildings does genuinely look a dangerous proposition.

The bomb-site battle that concludes *Hue and Cry* (1947)

Unlike the Ealing comedies of Robert Hamer and Alexander Mackendrick or indeed the black comedy of Crichton's film, *A Fish Called Wanda* (1988), the anarchic tendencies of *Hue and Cry* are soon subsumed under a tone of geniality and communal goodwill. Clarke and Crichton like a little fling but it is always counterbalanced by an inner desire for restraint and respect for the law. *Hue and Cry* does well in catching the humorous tone of a youthful prank: for example, it has a nice schoolboyish relish for rodent imagery, its rats and sewers anticipating such contemporary masterpieces as George Orwell's novel *1984* (1948) and Carol Reed's *The Third Man* (1949). It is a nice idea to have the credits chalked up on a wall like graffiti, but even here the comments are politely comic rather than cheekily subversive: 'Wot, no

124

producer' and 'King' alongside Crichton's name, for example. A rendition of 'O For the Wings of a Dove' in church at the beginning might be undercut by a shot of a boy as he reads his comic but the boys, albeit bruised and bandaged after their escapades, still return to the church at the end in a restoration of order. These are not the stuff of Dead End Kids: more the civil servants of the future.

THE YOUNG AND THE DAMNED – LOS OLVIDADOS
(Mexico 1951: Luis Buñuel)

Los Olvidados, which brought Luis Buñuel back to international prominence after nearly 20 years in the cinematic wilderness following the scandal of *L'Age d'Or* (1930), might seem to fit snugly into the mainstream of post-war screen realism. Its theme of childhood delinquency is reminiscent of de Sica's *Shoeshine*, a film Buñuel admired; and a scene where a young boy is accosted by an older man – innocence and yearning suddenly threatened by adult corruption – recalls a similar incident in de Sica's *Bicycle Thieves*. The film's prologue seems to relate childhood crime directly to social conditions and could almost have prefaced *Dead End*: 'Concealed behind the imposing structures of our great modern cities are pits of misery, hiding unwanted, hungry, dirty and uneducated children, a fertile breeding ground for future delinquents . . . .'[5]

But, being a film of Luis Buñuel, *Los Olvidados* does not take long to question the veracity of neo-realist techniques for their omission of the inner lives of its characters, and to scorn the social solutions offered by even the most well-meaning officials. Buñuel annihilates public pity and at one stage, when a young boy goes berserk at a farm school to which he has been sent for rehabilitation, even the camera lens is left with egg on its face . . . .

The film's main protagonists are Jaibo, a violent delinquent who will soon be sought for murder; Pedro, a sensitive boy with a problematical relationship with his mother; Big-Eyes, who has been separated from his father; and a blind man who takes Big-Eyes under his grubby wing. Of these the least sympathetic in Buñuel's vision is the blind man: 'Have pity on a poor blind man', he says. Yet pity is something that Buñuel scorns being, as he believes, the bourgeoisie's primary emotion of self-justification. Moreover, the blind man is in reality one of the least pitiable characters in movies: a police-informer, a would-be rapist, and an ostensibly helpless man whose white stick actually has a rusty nail on the end. When he hears the shooting that will kill Jaibo, he exults: 'One less! One less! They'll all end up the same way. They should all be killed before they're born!' His blindness is less a physical than a spiritual affliction, symptomatic of the kind of reactionary values Buñuel attacked all his life.

As Jaibo is dying, we hear a woman's voice-over ('As always, my son. As always. Goodnight'), presumably that of the mother he never knew; and we see a superimposition of a mangy dog walking into the darkness – like Jaibo, a prowling loner. If, in the film's elaborate associative montage, Jaibo is a mangy dog and the blind man is a haughty black cock, young Pedro is a helpless chicken, finally to die in a stable at the hands of Jaibo, a white hen standing on his chest. Earlier he has winced at the sight of his mother's killing of a hen, for it reminds him of having witnessed Jaibo's murder of an informer: it is an omen of his own fate. When he himself slaughters some chickens at the farm school, it seems a projection of the frustration and anger he feels at Jaibo and his mother, who have now begun an affair. However, far from punishing the boy, a kindly social worker attempts to understand ('That boy needs confidence and the affection he has never been given') and sends him out into society with some money. The moment is teasingly similar to that incident in *Oliver Twist* when Oliver, temporarily out of the clutches of Fagin and his gang, is encouraged by his benefactor, Brownlow, to re-enter society with some money entrusted to him. Both benefactors underrate the forces of fate and society, for they are sending their charges back into a corrupt world whose harsh reality cannot be changed simply by charity and good intentions alone.

Just as Oliver Twist will encounter Bill Sikes and Nancy, so Pedro will encounter Jaibo, who steals the money from him. Jaibo seems to operate as the nightmare side of Pedro's personality, for it is he who has stolen the knife and committed the crime for which Pedro has been detained and sent to the reformatory.

It is Jaibo who has stolen for a night the love of his mother, which Pedro has always craved but which has always been denied him (most spectacularly, in a dream sequence where the mother has offered him a dripping carcass as an emblem of her slavering contempt). Jaibo is a force of pure destruction in Pedro's life, rather like Orlick in Pip's in Dickens's *Great Expectations*: a symbol of his suppressed desires (for his mother) but also of the fearful fate that awaits him. Pedro's dead body will eventually be tipped out at dead of night on to a garbage heap, returning him to the wasteland from which the film started.

Los Olvidados is as unrelenting as the pitiless sun, heat and dust of the characters' surroundings and as harsh as the incomplete, metallic architecture of its environment. It is a particularly brutal portrayal of life in a modern city, but in addition to its Lawrentian indictment of modern urbanization, it also exposes old-fashioned attitudes that are rooted in ignorance, brutality and superstition. It is perhaps Buñuel's most scathing attack on the inhumanity of modern society, but it is all observed with a complete absence of sentimentality and a refusal to moralize: indeed, the judge who presumes to attack Pedro's mother for her behaviour to her son is roundly satirized. What is more, the film is teeming with sensuality, physicality and animal vitality, as desperate characters bare their talons in their fight to survive; and it is composed with wonderful quirkiness, even if Buñuel was not permitted to be quite as surrealistic as he would have liked. 'For instance, when Jaibo goes to beat up and kill the other boy', he said 'a camera movement reveals in the distance the framework of a huge 11-storey building under construction; I would have liked to put a big orchestra of a hundred musicians in it . . . .'[6] Fiddling while Mexico burns?

The influence of *Los Olvidados* can be seen in subsequent movies such as Hector Babenco's *Pixote* (1982) and Yilmaz Guney's *The Wall* (1984), which both detail the savagery of reformatories for homeless children and suggest them as a breeding-ground for childhood criminality — yet both are relatively ponderous pieces besides the exuberant, withering iconoclasm of Buñuel.

THE BAD NEWS BEARS

(USA 1976: Michael Ritchie)

'The ultimate anti-Disney movie'[7] said critic James Monaco of this film, whilst R. P. Kolker also cited it as one of the rare American movies that avoid the pitfalls of depicting childhood on screen: usually, he says, children 'exist either as small adults, or as unconscionably cute, or amazingly vicious'.[8] Here the children are depicted as a kind of corporate kid, an amazing ethnic mix that is made up of, as one of them sardonically puts it, 'Jews, spics, pansies and one booger-eating moron'. It is undoubtedly the profanity that distances these children from the Disney tradition, though the only four-letter word to which the team's coach, Buttermaker (Walter Matthau), takes violent exception is 'pill'. 'Don't ever say that word again!' he snaps at his star player, who happens to be a tomboy called Amanda (Tatum O'Neal).

Star player (Tatum O'Neal) and coach (Walter Matthau) survey their sorry team in *The Bad News Bears* (1976)

The Bad News Bears are the worst baseball team in the Little League, and much of their badness is attributable to the example set by their coach, Buttermaker, who is a cynical alcoholic and rumpled reprobate. However,

needled by the arrogant criticism of a rival coach, Turner (Vic Morrow), Buttermaker changes tactics and drafts in two excellent players, a motor-cycle delinquent (Jack Haley Jnr) and Amanda, who is the daughter of one of Buttermaker's ex-girlfriends. The fortunes of the team dramatically improve and they meet Turner's team in the League final, a crucial game that will occupy the last half-hour of the film.

Beneath the slapstick and the satire, *The Bad News Bears* is a film bristling with ideas. It surveys the pressure of the success syndrome on America's children, with baseball becoming a metaphor for competitiveness and even life itself. Significantly, the film's action takes place almost exclusively on the baseball park, with no scenes at home or at school. It casts a quizzical sideways glance at the place of girls in this all-American pursuit, and implicitly, the future of women in this kind of American society. It scathingly surveys the way adults either project their own fantasies on to children in their charge, as Turner does, or infect them with their own sense of failure, as Buttermaker does. 'Look at yourself, look at that team', says Turner contemptuously to Buttermaker: the team is a reflection *on* him and a reflection of him, and its improved performance is in direct ratio to his growing self-respect. Conversely, Turner begins to confuse his team's success with his own ambitions and pride and, at a key moment in the final, strikes his son. At which point Buttermaker decides to pull out his two best players and give everyone a go: winning cannot be worth that much. Implicitly, it is a decision to let them stay in the realm of childhood play a little longer. The world of cut-throat competitiveness will be upon them soon enough.

If the film is overtly about America, whose values it examines with an ironic eye, it is also about democracy, where baseball now becomes a metaphor for playing according to the rules: for integration and assimilation into a team (society); and for channelling one's energies for the common, rather than individual, good. If this all sounds suspiciously Disneyesque, it would be as well here to list the differences: Matthau's rough-diamond hero (rather than say, Fred MacMurray's boy-scout in a Disney film); the fringe observations of commercialism; the strong language as an index of the kid's undomesticated rebelliousness; the unresolved relationship between But-termaker and Amanda where her subtle attempt to ingratiate herself as a possible future daughter triggers off in him a frightening eruption of rage and rejection; the theme of parents and teachers asking too much of their young, as the coaches in the dug-outs roar at their charges like animals in a cage; and the heroism of the loser. 'It's not a Disney movie, yet it's the kind of movie I hope will make the audience feel good in the end', said director Michael Ritchie. It certainly does and not because of a spoonful of sugar, but because of a salty dose of realism and intelligence.

Stand By Me
(USA 1986: Rob Reiner)
River's Edge
(USA 1986: Tim Hunter)

Stand by Me and *River's Edge* are two of the most interesting and challenging of recent 'teen' movies and could almost be seen as mirror images of each other. Both are based to a certain extent on true stories – the former a selective recollection of his childhood by Stephen King, the latter about an actual incident when a young man murdered his 14-year-old girlfriend for seemingly no reason. Both films are about friendship, group loyalty and teenage morality, though dealing with these themes in a very different way. Both have a dual perspective of past and present. Although set predominantly in 1959, *Stand by Me* is structured as a memory in the present of a writer (Richard Dreyfuss) looking back at his 12-year-old self. Although set in the 1980s, *River's Edge* has the ghost of the 1960s clinging to it, particularly in the form of a post-*Easy Rider* Dennis Hopper. Both plots begin with a body. Ironically, although *Stand by Me* is based on a story by the King of modern horror fiction, it is *River's Edge* that is much the more horrific.

Looking for a body in *Stand By Me* (1986): from left to right, Will Wheaton, River Phoenix, Jerry O'Connell and Corey Feldman

Based on King's story 'The Body', *Stand by Me* tells of a gang of four boys who go searching for a body in the woods. One of them has overheard his brothers talking of having discovered it and going back to claim the reward. On their journey, they have a number of exciting adventures, notably when two of them are nearly run over by a train or when another is almost savaged by a dump keeper's dog. They also pour out their souls and, at the last stage, are threatened by an older quartet who represent a debased form of the

group some years hence, shadowing the leads and trying to claim the body for themselves.

The macabre nature of the expedition is perhaps the most characteristic Stephen King element, although there are other features that one has come to recognize as typical of his work, most notably the tensions of home life and the refusal to reassert the wholeness of the family at the story's end. Also a story by the main character, Gordie (Will Wheaton), which he invents for his friends, about a fat boy who takes revenge on all those who have mocked him, resembles King's hit novel, *Carrie*.

Gordie is clearly meant to represent a youthful King, showing the stirrings of early literary creativity and exhibiting an anxiety and sensitivity that set him slightly apart from the rest of the group. (It is significant that it is he who is privileged with the one moment of beauty in the film, when he encounters a deer as it gracefully emerges from out of the wood.) Nevertheless he is a more active figure in the film than in the story, pointing a gun at the leader of the older gang (Kiefer Sutherland) when the latter is threatening his friend Chris (River Phoenix).

The rawness of childhood language and the intricacies of the group interaction are neatly observed, and the acting and comic writing have some very pleasurable moments. 'If Mickey was a mouse, Donald was a duck and Pluto a dog ... what's Goofy?' asks Gordie in genuine bewilderment; and *Wagon Train* is discussed as 'a really good show, but did you notice they never get anywhere?' Their journey inevitably takes the form of a fall from innocence, and the undercurrents of violence, the literal sense in the tale of 'have gun, will travel', make it a very American rite of passage. Two main themes emerge. The first comes after the discovery that the guard dog on the dump, Chopper, with the reputation of being a Baskerville hound that devours your private parts, is actually not a raging Cujo but a mangy mongrel. 'Chopper', says Gordie, 'was my first lesson in the difference between myth and reality': one might say it is his first step on the road to adulthood. The second theme is the comment by a middle-aged Gordie (Dreyfuss) whose remembrance of that day has been stirred by reading in the paper of the death of one of his friends. 'I never had any friends like the ones I had when I was 12', he muses. 'Jesus, did anyone?'

King's nostalgic attitude to childhood makes a sharp contrast to the unnerving attitudes revealed in *River's Edge*, which could be seen as a dark-hearted parody of *Stand by Me* (whereas in *Stand by Me* a sensitive 12-year-old is traumatized by the death of his beloved elder brother, in *River's Edge* a murderous 12-year-old is at one stage prepared to kill his). A corpse is once again at the centre of the story, hidden by woods, but this time the murderer is amongst them, a friend, as was the victim. This lugubrious state of affairs triggers off all kinds of confusions in the undeveloped minds of a gang who have basically learnt about loyalty from Chuck Norris movies and *Starsky and Hutch*. Their moral sense is virtually non-existent. Yet these are not dead-end but high-school kids, the new bland generation, perhaps the product of a species of amoral adulthood whose emergence so flabbergasted Arthur Miller when he gave a lecture on morality and science: 'I was surrounded by 20 or 30 women who were not at all satisfied that drowning people was not science and wanted further explanation. This was the first

The face of alienated youth in *River's Edge* (1986)

time I had faced Cool, the truthfulness without truth, the blandly interested post-humanist faces.'[9]

If *River's Edge* is the *Easy Rider* of the 1980s one should add that these kids are spaced-out, not drop-outs, and their mood is not one of anger and protest but apathy and paranoia. Parents are just voices off ('Clarissa, is that you?'); education seems pointless and alienating; the apocalypse is anticipated. The mood is unremittingly nihilistic.

'There was a meaning in the madness', says the teacher to these kids about the 1960s. A former flower-child, he now berates the present generation on their indifference to everything and their lack of concern or commitment. When he tries to provoke the class into discussing the motiveless murder of their friend, the only response he gets is: 'Are we gonna be tested on this stuff?' Sometimes the disjunction between horrific event and bland reaction verges on surreal black comedy, and the film becomes a youth movie *Trouble with Harry*.

Dennis Hopper as the town madman, Feck, is on hand to afford some perspective. He lives with a life-sized mannequin, an intriguing correlative to the doll with which the film has opened: it is during the act of throwing his sister's rag doll maliciously into the river that young Tim (Joshua Miller) has first seen the hulking murderer Samson (Daniel Roebuck) sitting beside

131

the body of his dead girlfriend. We learn that Feck has also murdered his woman in the past, but whereas he has misguidedly killed out of love – there was a meaning in his madness – Samson has killed out of, at best, a kind of alienated indifference. His friend Layne (Crispin Glover) tries to elevate it into an act of heroism, but he is a mannered maniac who is more interested in show than substance, his loyalty being more performance than reality.

'The sadness of *River's Edge*', says Tim Hunter, 'comes from the real lack of intellectual resources that these kids have with which to make their own decisions and build their own lives. They just don't know a goddamned thing. They don't read. They're not educated. They have no sense of culture or history.'[10] One thinks of *Back to the Future*, when an American youth is transported back to the 1950s and, astonishingly, has no idea where he is. Whose fault is it? The film has no clear-cut answers, or rights and wrongs. Is it the youngsters, the schools, the parents, society, government? Clearly what the youngsters see is a society with no future (the bomb is going to drop), so education has little meaning to them; and if they are living entirely in and for the present, there is frighteningly little moral restraint, particularly when, as Hunter puts it, 'they see their government more interested in bombs than in education, more interested in international debt than individual communities'. Unlike *Stand by Me*, where the gang is a mini-society, with a rough sense of civic morality and responsibility, the gang in *River's Edge* is anti-society, an amorphous rag-bag of quirkily individualist values, roughly indicating group loyalty but actually pointing the way to total chaos. Fifty years on, the tide has turned. These are devils, not angels, with dirty faces.

CHAPTER SEVEN

BLUE REMEMBERED HILLS

Into my heart an air that kills
From your far country blows:
What are those blue remembered hills,
What spires, what farms are those?

That is the land of lost content,
I see it shining plain,
The happy highways where I went
And cannot come again

             (A. E. HOUSMAN, *A Shropshire Lad*)

Rosebud . . .

             (*Citizen Kane*)

IN the cinema, the path back to childhood is strewn with either rosebuds or deadly nightshades. Childhood is the past, a foreign country, often – as in *The Go-Between*, *The Railway Children* and Peter Weir's *Picnic at Hanging Rock* (1975) – recollected in bright sunshine as a Golden Age. Yet it is approached along two roads marked nostalgia and disillusionment. Nostalgia is stimulated by a yearning for the former innocence of childhood, the security of parental love, the sense of life as a game, and the freedom to indulge in recklessness rather than be inhibited by the bonds of responsibility.

As we shall see in the films discussed, the disillusionment comes at the moment when one or all of these things is lost: when the sophisticated deceits of adulthood become dangerous; when the early stirrings of sexuality bring jealousy and confusion in their wake; when songs of innocence become laments of experience.

CITIZEN KANE

(USA 1941 : Orson Welles)

It might seem odd to feature *Citizen Kane* prominently in a book on childhood, since there is only one scene of childhood in it. However, it could be argued that this is the most important scene in one of the cinema's most important movies.

There is a famous 'Peanuts' cartoon by Schulz in the *Los Angeles Times* in which Linus's first viewing of *Citizen Kane* is spoilt when Lucy blurts out: 'Rosebud was his sled!' But of course, 'Rosebud' – the dying word of Kane (Orson Welles), the significance of which the rest of the film seeks to decipher – is more than just his sled. It is the word that, for Kane, summons up the whole of his childhood and indeed, just as the sled will be consumed in flames almost simultaneously with our discovery of the meaning of 'Rosebud', so will Kane's chilhood be summarily concluded almost before it has begun. As André Bazin puts it: 'Kane admits before dying that there is no profit in gaining the whole world if one has lost one's childhood.'[1]

The revelation of 'Rosebud' inevitably forces us to reconsider the significance of the scene in which the young Charles Foster Kane is signed away by his mother (Agnes Moorehead) to be cared for by a guardian, Thatcher (George Coulouris), who is to look after his financial affairs. It is something of a mystery in the film why the mother chooses to send her son away. There is a suggestion that she is aiming to get him away from the contaminating influence of his drunken, ineffectual father. However, her father's explanation is that, 'Your Ma figures – well, that is, me and her decided this ain't the place for you to grow up in. You'll probably be the richest man in America someday, and you ought to get an education.' These reasons are probably meant to mystify young Kane, and all he picks up, which is to be crucial in his development, is a sense of the conflicting ties of money and feelings. His wealth is separating him from his mother's love.

Although the scene is recalled in Thatcher's memoirs, which the reporter is reading, the visual prominence of Kane's mother makes it seem more like Kane's own dying recollection. He plays outside in the snow on his sled 'Rosebud' whilst, unbeknown to him, inside his fate is being sealed. Subsequently, he will attack Thatcher with his sled (in essence, pitting his childhood and innocence against Thatcher's values of conservatism and commercialism); and it is significant that, when Thatcher as an old man asks Kane what he would most like to have been, Kane's reply brings back the feeling of that childhood attack: 'Everything you hate.'

As well as the sled, the snow forms part of Kane's nostalgic recollection of this scene, a nostalgia for snow often seeming a characteristic of childhood memories and fantasies (from Cocteau's *Les Enfants Terribles* to Raymond Briggs's *The Snowman*). In his first meeting with the lady who will become his second wife, Susan Alexander (Dorothy Comingore), he will notice she has in her apartment one of those ornamental glass balls of snow that has within it a miniature house, which recalls the log cabin where he lived as a child. Later, when she leaves him and he wrecks her room in rage – a room which itself looks more like a doll's house than that of a mature, respected wife – the one item he spares is this glass snowball, the sight of which will once again trigger a memory of 'Rosebud'.

Picnic at Hanging Rock
(1975)

135

Indeed, the whole relationship with Susan seems intimately connected with Kane's sense of a lost childhood. They first meet when he says he was undertaking a journey back to the past 'in search of my youth'. She brings out something of the child in him: he entertains her with schoolboy tricks, like wiggling his ears and doing shadow graphs on the walls. He also senses something of a kindred spirit. Like Kane, Susan has been forced into a pathway of life (her mother's ambitions for her as a singer) that will destroy her; both submit to the wishes of a parent figure whom they love. 'You know what mothers are like', says Susan, to which Kane replies quietly, 'Yes'. It is practically the only time he alludes to his mother in the entire film but, although he rarely talks of her, her influence is felt in the way he sometimes talks like her. 'I want you to stop this, Susan', he says to her in their tent, attempting to cut short her complaining; and one suddenly flashes back to the childhood scene when Kane Snr has been grumbling about the arrangements for his son's future, and Mrs Kane says briefly, 'I want you to stop all this nonsense, Jim . . .'

Thatcher (George Coulouris) shakes hands with the young Kane (Buddy Swann), clutching his sled, in *Citizen Kane* (1941): father (Harry Shannon) and mother (Agnes Moorehead) look on

136

Perhaps the loss of sensitivity that goes with his lost childhood is signified most strongly in the film by the presentation of Kane's only child by his first marriage, a son. The boy will be killed in a motor accident, but his death will only be alluded to by a newspaper headline, and Kane himself will never refer to it. The reason for this is perhaps that the boy is, like the boy's mother, more a constituent of Kane's political ambitions than of his tenderest feelings. (The boy's comment at Kane's political rally – 'Is Daddy Governor yet?' – neatly underlines that: strangely, this moment does not appear in the film's published shooting script.) Rather than the boy, it is Susan whom Kane seems to see as his potential substitute 'Rosebud'. On her opera début, we notice that she picks up a rose from the stage, which is almost certainly tossed by Kane, since no one else cares for her singing. Yet he destroys her through money and ambition in the way that he has been destroyed. 'Rosebud', then, is a complex reference in the film, partly the Wellesian 'McGuffin' in a psychological detective story, but also a recollection of childhood and the loss of a mother's love; and a symbol of frustrated romanticism in Kane that, because of this emotionally frozen beginning to his life, has been nipped in the bud and thereafter can never find expression.

THE FALLEN IDOL
(GB 1948 : Carol Reed)

Adapted by Graham Greene from his short story 'The Basement Room', *The Fallen Idol* tells the story of a young boy, Felipe (Bobby Henrey), who is the son of the French Ambassador in London. Felipe hero-worships the Ambassador's valet and butler, Baines (Ralph Richardson), particularly in preference to the abrasive and embittered Mrs Baines (Sonia Dresdel), who seems to despise their relationship. His loyalty is to be tested when he mistakenly believes that Baines has pushed his wife to her death.

In the film, the child is doubly an outsider: as a foreigner in England, and as a child in a mysterious adult world. Both will serve to amplify his misconception of events. By showing so much of the film through the child's eyes (point-of-view shots as he looks down the stairs, low-angle shots of adults), director Carol Reed emphasizes the limitations of the young boy's viewpoint. This will contribute crucially to the effectiveness of the central drama of the film – the death of Mrs Baines – where he fails to see precisely what occurs but jumps to conclusions on the basis of this inadequate knowledge. The boy's lack of understanding of the adult machinations going on around him was very carefully nurtured by Reed, who only told him little scraps of the plot when it suited his needs and filmed him separately from the other actors for much of the time.

When Felipe blunders into the tea-room, disturbing Baines and his 'niece' Julie (Michelle Morgan), he little realizes that he is blundering into a love affair: it is almost like Carol Reed's private joke on the famous opening scene of *Brief Encounter* (1945) by his great rival, David Lean. Baines will later contrive a visit to the zoo with Felipe, which, unbeknown to the boy, is really a pretext for a further meeting with Julie. The setting becomes unusually expressive. It is a fleeting reminder of Felipe's pet snake, which Mrs Baines has destroyed: she will find the serpent of her husband's adultery harder to dismiss. The shots of Felipe behind the bars of a cage not only emphasize the limits of his vision but imply childhood as a kind of prison. Finally the zoo setting will serve as a forewarning of predatory adult passions that are soon to break free of their cages. Of all the directors who have inherited Reed's great gifts and influence, the most talented is probably Jack Clayton, and there is a kind of homage to this zoo scene in Clayton's *The Pumpkin Eater* (1964), where two adults meet at a zoo and, against a background of animal shrieks and childhood innocence, adulterous jealousies give rise to animalistic anger.

Later, in a scene that will anticipate a similar scene in Clayton's *The Innocents*, Baines, Julie and Felipe will be alone in the Embassy and will play a game of 'Hide-and-Seek-in-the-Dark', which, Greene tells us in his autobiography, *A Sort of Life*, was one of his favourite childhood games – 'containing the agreeable ingredient of fear.'[2] As in Clayton's film, the game precipitates the terrifying appearance of a ghost, or so Felipe thinks. It is actually Mrs Baines, who is hiding in the Embassy to catch out the lovers. Her frightening appearance before Felipe is signified by a simple yet chilling image that is borrowed from the story – a hairpin dropping on the child's pillow, like a fat spider, when he is just about to sleep. The stage is set for the violent confrontation between husband and wife, and the fall that will send Felipe running in terror through the night streets.

From here the film will wind down the tension most adroitly, and will gradually become a sort of comedy of non-communication. The shift of tone is signalled by a superb scene in a police station where Felipe has been taken. He is befriended by a prostitute (Dora Bryan) who, when asked by the police to try and get some information out of the lad, cannot help lapsing into ingrained habits: 'Hello, dearie, where do you live?' 'Can't you do it without the smile?' asks the policeman on the desk wearily. It is an interesting shift from the story, where this function was taken by a rather dour, colourless policewoman. The film's characterization is both livelier and more appropriate. The prostitute is a reminder of the sexual motives at the heart of the film that have led to the event that has so disorientated Felipe, but also a beautifully played comic type that ushers in the film's new tone. In the final part of the film, rather as in the role of the girl in the trial scene of Mackendrick's *A High Wind in Jamaica*, the child's attempt to help the adult he really cares for only serves to incriminate him still further. This chain of failed communications is strengthened further by exasperating distractions – deadly investigation being interrupted by the arrival of the cleaners, and by the clock-winder – and by objects and clues that keep changing form and significance, like a crucial crumpled telegram that Felipe converts into a paper dart, only inadvertently to direct it like a poisoned arrow to land at a police inspector's feet. Finally the mess is cleared up and the details of the accident clarified, but not before Felipe has been disillusioned about Baines (it seems his stories about his exploits in Africa were a complete fabrication) and totally exasperated by adult indifference: 'Now will somebody please listen to me . . .'

It is a film that plays some very sophisticated games on the thin line that separates 'secrets' from 'lies' – secrets that can be fun or can be fatal, lies that can be kindness but can also be deception. It contrasts the secret world of

Bobby Henrey, Michele Morgan and Ralph Richardson in the tearoom scene in *The Fallen Idol* (1948)

childhood, which is expressed in fantasy, with the secret world of adulthood, which is expressed here, and often elsewhere, in infidelity. But it is interesting to compare the film with the much darker original story, which concerns a small boy who unwittingly betrays his best friend to the police. The story is structured as a death-bed flashback to childhood, triggered by a particular phrase – rather in the manner of 'Rosebud' in *Citizen Kane*. It is the story of an embittered 60-year-old who, towards the end of his life, recollects the traumatic event of his youth that destroyed the people dearest to him – 'Life fell on him with savagery, and you could't blame him if he never faced it again in 60 years'.[3] Reed chose not to make that story, but it seems a remarkable premonition of Joseph Losey's film of L. P. Hartley's *The Go-Between*, which, if not about fallen idols, is certainly about fallen angels: 'You flew too near the sun, and you were scorched'.

139

A HIGH WIND IN JAMAICA
(GB 1965: Alexander Mackendrick)

This is one of those happy occasions where a fine book has found its ideal interpreter. Richard Hughes's novel, first published in 1929, is a story of children being kidnapped by pirates. The twist is that the pirates become much more afraid of the children than the other way round – as Hughes puts it, the children 'were treated with a detached severity not wholly divorced from fear – as if these unfortunate men at last realized what diabolic yeast had been introduced into their lump'.[4] The book explores the gap between adult and child, the incomprehension and danger that can arise from the incomplete understanding of each other's world, culminating in the execution of the pirate captain through the innocent testimony of a young girl.

The adaptation follows the novel quite closely, with some interesting variations. The killing of the Dutch captain by Emily and the arrest of the pirates are telescoped into a single sustained incident. Captain Chavez's fascination with Emily (from his first appearance when their eyes meet) is given more emphasis and sexuality in the film than the novel. Because of the sensitive peformances of Anthony Quinn and Deborah Baxter, this relationship is handled with great tact and feeling, and is the emotional heart of the film. In the film, the tension between the worlds of adult and child is particularly brought out in the attitude to games: a monkey falls to its death when an adult crew member behaves childishly and gets drunk; a child (a young Martin Amis) falls to his death when he becomes over-interested in adult sports and slips from his perch attempting to lean over for a better view. John's death is treated somewhat differently in the novel (he is watching the attempt to retrieve a cow and loses his balance), and the film's endeavour with this detail to sharpen the tension between the adult and the child world seems intelligent and successful. The theme is expanded in a wonderfully sustained sequence (not in the novel) where a game with the captain's hat subtly and unwittingly starts the process whereby his authority with his crew is slowly undermined, and a game with the ship's figurehead terrifies the superstitious crew. The figurehead is tossed like a ball but bounces and then shudders still on the deck like a skull, an emissary of death. It is as if the children have now cast a spell on the crew and only disaster can ensue.

The last 20 minutes of the picture touch a high peak of excitement. The pirate captain has been locked up by his mutinous crew as they attack the Dutch ship. Emily, recuperating from an accident, is terrified by the sudden distorted appearance of the Dutch captain in Chavez's cabin, misinterprets his garbled request to be cut free from his bonds and stabs him to death. Chavez stumbles upon the murder prior to his arrest, powerless to prevent the killing but seeing what has happened. In England the children are questioned and the misinterpretations begin to multiply. The adults seize suspiciously on the disclosure that Chavez used the word 'drawers' whereas, in the actual context, he was remonstrating with the children to act with a bit more demure decency.

The theme of the film and novel is the journey towards English values. This was the original reason why the children were sent home. On the pirate ship, however, they have discovered a dangerous vitality and, by the time they reach England, they feel even further alienated from the values of decency and restraint that actually seem to represent a repression of natural instincts. When an impeccably dressed Emily enters that repository of English standards, the courtroom, the camera movement (keeping her face in tight close-up) thrusts an awareness of her confusion and agitation very forcefully towards us. She is much more frightened by the lawyer than by the pirates. With the sound of public opinion providing a dismal moral accompaniment, Emily's testimony unwittingly sends the pirate captain to the gallows. She tells the truth but the pronouns became confused: 'He (the pirate captain, Chavez) gave me medicine . . . to make me sleep. . . . He (the Dutch captain) had a knife', and the dark adult interpretation of her words sweeps like a tide towards an irresistible guilty verdict. 'I don't want to die innocent', cries the mate (James Coburn) to which Chavez replies, laughingly ironically, 'Zac, you must be guilty of something.' Tainted innocence, qualified guilt. In the novel, Emily is last seen at her new school, making friends, the experience perhaps behind her. In the film, the father looks over, uncomprehendingly, as Emily watches a toy boat sailing across a lake, perhaps permanently traumatized by the memory of the adult she loved and whose death she caused. Ostensibly she is back safe in the bosom of her family in England (again one notes the suffocating clothes as a

The killing of the Dutch captain in *A High Wind in Jamaica* (1965): Gert Frobe as the captain, Deborah Baxter as the young girl.

metaphor for moral oppression) but her heart is clearly elsewhere, haunted by the ghost of the pirate captain and perhaps also by her murder of the Dutch captain. The novel's concluding diminuendo is a delicate, tentative reaffirmation of innocence. The film's ending has the sombre atmosphere of an impending storm and the phrase in the air is that of the pirate – 'You must be guilty of something . . .'

WALKABOUT
(GB/Australia 1970: Nicolas Roeg)

It is interesting to compare *High Wind in Jamaica* with Nicolas Roeg's film of *Walkabout*. Both are about British children in an alien environment searching to find their way back to 'civilization' and social decorum. Both are encounters between a sexually burgeoning girl and a free spirit – in one case, a pirate, in the other an Aborigine – whose love for the girl uncovers a dissatisfaction with his natural life and is ultimately to lead to death by hanging. In both films the endings bring the works full circle, with both girls back at home with loved ones, but both given an enigmatic finale where they wistfully summon up an image from the past – a regret for the loss of naturalness, of childhood innocence and independence, and perhaps for lost love. Roeg saw his film essentially as one concerning identity and destiny: 'They had everything to offer each other (i.e. the girl and the Aborigine), but they couldn't communicate and went zooming to their own separate destinies through the odd placement of identity, the identity that other people had put on them. The girl came nearly to the point where she could have changed but then in one moment when they see the road, she slipped all the way back, tumbled back into this mould. So nearly . . . and there was still doubt in her right at the end of the film.'[5]

The girl (Jenny Agutter) and her younger brother (Lucien John) have been stranded in the Australian desert after their father (John Meillon) has driven them out for a picnic, tried to kill them but then turned the gun upon himself. Prior to this disturbing event – the eruption of death into a child's game will also figure in the opening of Roeg's next film, *Don't Look Now* (1973) – we have been given an oblique introduction to the characters and their lives, which is of great significance in the context of later development: a sense of the pressure of city life, the uniformity of school routine, and the familiarity of family relationships that are imperceptibly hardening into indifference. In one particular shot, Roeg pans along a city wall to reveal the desert in the background, an image that has implications about man's inner desolation and the savage that lurks inside civilized man. Perhaps most of all, it evokes D. H. Lawrence's phrase about the 'glimpse beyond the walled city' that, in Lawrence's view, is the tragic catalyst for the fate of Thomas Hardy's main characters. The glimpse arouses a dissatisfaction with the limitations of the walled city but those who venture beyond it inevitably carry its values with them, which might jeopardize their survival.

The children's survival is initially in doubt as, incongruously dressed in their school uniforms, they make their trek across the wilderness. Far from being deserted, the desert will turn out to be crackling with life, as the animal world surveys this invasion of its territory. Roeg's nature filming is wonderful here, transforming the creatures into dragons and monsters that

Asking the Aborigine for water: David Gumpilil (left) Lucien John (centre) and Jenny Agutter (right) in *Walkabout* (1970)

are the fitting inhabitants of a child's adventure. The appearance of a snake and a wombat while the children sleep indicates the potential of the desert for menace and charm; and one great shot of the sleeping boy dissolves a close-up of his face into the texture of a rock, as if the rock, in a momentary assertion of harmony between humanity and its surroundings, has softened into a pillow.

The appearance of the Aborigine (David Gumpilil) on his walkabout will have the effect of turning their perceptions upside down. To begin with, it will further the contrast between the girl, who is now more mother than big sister, and her brother, which has been concisely established in two lines of dialogue:

GIRL: We don't want people thinking we're a couple of tramps.
BOY: What people?

It is not surprising, then, that initially the boy can communicate much more easily with the Aborigine than the girl. Being older, she is over-sophisticated and relies on language. Her brother is more instinctive and relies on mime, to much greater effect. As the Aborigine teaches them the art of survival in the desert, Roeg crosscuts to the clumsy, brutal 'real' world (ogling males at a weather station, the butcher chopping his meat) and delicately the themes of primitivism and civilization, liberation and oppression, instinct and mechanization, are adumbrated. It will end at the discovery of the road; the girl's taking flight at the Aborigine's courtship dance; and a return to rude civilization, in which the first exhortation to the re-born children is, 'Don't *touch* anything . . .'

The action of the film is framed by two suicides – the father and the Aborigine – which are both mysterious, take the children by surprise, and take place in a kind of no man's land between city and desert. The fact that they are inexplicable is consistent with the children's view: it adds a dimension of enigma and terror to their experience and their sense of the ultimate unknowability of people. Yet there are hints about the motives behind both deaths. In the father's case there is a suggestion of the eruption of the savage in man (he does seem to pose a momentary sexual threat to his daughter), but also of a man confined and repressed by his city life, a classic victim of the Freudian discontents of civilization. In the Aborigine's case, there is a sense that the suicide is an acknowledgement of himself as an anachronism – natural man in a mechanized world. His dance might begin as a hopeful courtship ritual (a plea for integration or, more probably, for the girl to join him in his natural world), but it soon becomes a dance of death, a premonition of which has been suggested by the shot of his lying amongst the skeletons of slaughtered animals.

The final scene of the film leaps forward a few years. The girl is now a young wife, in the kitchen as her husband returns home from the office – a rather creepy reminiscence of the film's opening domestic scenes of her mother and father. She is surrounded by mechanical appliances, and our attention is particularly drawn to her heavy eye make-up (the triumph of the artificial over the natural, a civilized war-paint). Yet, as her husband speaks, she looks away wistfully and imagines a paradisal scene where she, her brother and the Aborigine bathe naked in a clear stream, their school uniforms left standing on a stick like forlorn scarecrows. As she imagines this, the words of the poet A. E. Housman are spoken over the soundtrack:

> That is the land of lost content,
> I see it shining plain,
> The happy highways where I went
> And cannot come again.

It is a lament for the loss of childhood naturalness and independence, and seems to refer not only to an ideal past but also to a failed future. Blake and Lawrence would have understood.

THE GO-BETWEEN
(GB 1970: Joseph Losey)

Adapted by Harold Pinter from the L. P. Hartley novel, *The Go-Between* is a tale about the golden summer of 1900 in the life of a 12-year-old boy, Leo (Dominic Guard), who is holidaying at the house of a well-to-do schoolfriend. Leo unwittingly becomes a go-between for his friend's elder sister, Marian (Julie Christie), and the local farmer, Ted Burgess (Alan Bates), with whom Marian is secretly having an affair. The situation begins to darken as Leo becomes increasingly friendly with Marian's fiancé, Lord Trimingham (Edward Fox), and as Leo's role in the Marian/Burgess affair begins to be suspected by Marian's mother, Mrs Maudsley (Margaret Leighton). Things come to a head at Leo's birthday party at which Marian is expected but is mysteriously missing. In the pouring rain, Mrs Maudsley drags Leo with her to look for Marian, clearly knowing that she will find her with Ted Burgess.

The final part of the film has tremendous impact largely because of the intensity of the performances of Michael Redgrave (playing the 60-year-old Leo looking back on these traumatic events) and Margaret Leighton as Mrs Maudsley. In the elder Leo's reunion with Marian, Redgrave's acting is particularly superb, conveying naked terror when Marian tries to persuade him to intercede on behalf of her grandson who believes he is under some sort of curse (a legacy of Leo's childhood interest in witchcraft?). Also, whereas in the novel Leo is going to deliver Marian's final message to Burgess's grandson in a spirit of reconciliation, in the film Redgrave's flint-like face eloquently says that he is not. Indeed, considering that the opening and closing of the film are the same (the rain beating on the window of the elder Leo's limousine), it is possible to see the whole film as his reverie as he sits immobile in the car, remembering the past, wondering what to do, flitting between past and present in his mind, and clearly still as much traumatized by the event now as he was at the time. Yet, considering he has known about Ted and Marian's affair sometime earlier, why has the event had such an impact on him? It cannot be Burgess's subsequent suicide, since neither the novel ('for the tidings of Ted's suicide came to me voicelessly, like a communication in a dream'), nor the film (a brief subjective flashback of Ted slumped at a table, the gun by his side, a small pool of blood) gives it much emphasis. The reason for Leo's trauma must lie somewhere else.

The reason is surely connected to the biggest mystery of both novel and film: why Mrs Maudsley chooses to take Leo with her to the outhouse. She says she needs him to show her the way but, in the event, she leads and he follows, so this is clearly not the case. It might be that Hartley realized she would have to take Leo with her because the novel required her to do so: in other words, in plot terms, Leo has to be there because he is the narrator and has to be able to recount what happened. The novelist's problem then is to come up with a psychologically plausible explanation to justify Mrs Maudsley's behaviour, since this action (particularly as she knows full well what they will find) seems to have a perverted cruelty to it that cannot adequately be explained by an outraged sense of social decorum. Curiously, Hartley offers no real explanation for it. He invites us to infer that she intends it as a kind of punishment but, if so, it is a punishment out of all proportion to the crime, since she has suspected something is going on long before Leo appears on the scene: he may have facilitated the romance, but he certainly has not initiated it. In fact, at this point, it is clear that Mrs Maudsley is completely out of control, which is the reason that her husband shouts out her name, 'Madeleine!' for the one and only time: it might startle this temporarily 'mad' woman into some form of restraint.

Again, although the novel does not spell it out, it is implied that Leo's most fearful memory of that whole incident is not the suicide nor the betrayal nor even the sex but Mrs Maudsley's reaction and behaviour on that night. It is the thing that the narrator Leo emphasizes most, at an early stage in Chapter Two when he is remembering Mrs Maudsley ('when I see her in dreams – for I have not been able to keep her out of them – it is not with that terrible aspect she wore the last time I saw her, when her face could hardly be called a face at all . . .') and in the Epilogue ('I had betrayed them all – Lord Trimingham, Ted, Marian, the whole Maudsley family who had welcomed me into their midst. Just what the consequences had been I neither knew nor wished to know; I judged their seriousness by Mrs Maudsley's screams, which were the last sounds heard by my conscious ear . . .') Hartley does not follow through the implications of all this, but the film, aided by Margaret Leighton's remarkable performance, does. There is only one thing that makes people behave as dementedly as that and it is not class outrage but sexual jealousy.

After all, if the revelation is a sexual one, why should not the motive be that also? And how does Mrs Maudsley know exactly where to go, if she has not been in that outhouse with Burgess herself? In the film, Margaret Leighton's intense performance only really makes sense as the performance of a rejected woman who has been thrown over by her lover for her daughter. The three seem intimately connected at numerous stages in the film, particularly in the way that all three of them, initially kind to Leo, turn on him ferociously at a later stage. The difference is that whereas he has been deceived and betrayed by Marian and Ted, whom he loved, he has been deceived by Mrs Maudsley whom he fears and who forces him to look at the most intimate joyous physical contact as if he is staring into the face of evil itself.

Why is the material of *The Go-Between* by far the most powerful of all the traditional 'rites of passage' works? Partly it has to do with the extreme skill with which it works its variations on prior literary classics. Like Henry James's *The Turn of the Screw*, it is concerned with children who are

146

Marian turns on Leo: Julie Christie and Dominic Guard in *The Go-Between* (1970)

destroyed by the sexual neuroses of their parents and guardians. In one sense, Leo could be identified with James's governess in the tale. Like her, he tries to exorcise the evil ('Die ... die ... all evil', says Leo in the film, when he is tearing out the roots of the deadly nightshade). Like the governess, in so doing he destroys some of the people he most loves and consigns himself to a life of emptiness. Equally like the governess in a Freudian reading of the tale is Mrs Maudsley, a sexual neurotic who terrifies a child into looking at an 'evil' he simply cannot recognize as such, and in the process consigns him to a living death. One suspects also that Hartley was much influenced by one of the greatest of all novels about childhood, Dickens's *Great Expectations*. Both novels have a dual vision of a childhood being simultaneously experienced and reflected upon, so that the narrator not only relives the action but also comments on it with the benefit of hindsight and from the perspective of maturity. Like Dickens's Pip, Leo will be traumatized by his brief encounter with upper-class society. Like Dickens's Estella, Marian is a spoilt heroine who teases and destroys the boy who loves her. And like Dickens's Miss Havisham, Mrs Maudsley is the seeming benefactress who seems part of Leo's great expectations, but who,

147

sexually thwarted, becomes the wicked witch who will break his heart.

When novels and films deploy this dual perspective on childhood – that is, childhood revisited and reviewed from an adult perspective – the dominant theme is often not childhood itself but memory, regret, and a lament for lost innocence. If *The Go-Between* is one of the most powerful examples of the genre, the reason is that innocence and memory are such complicated issues in the story for Leo, who has mixed feelings about them. Certainly he has nostalgia for that Golden Age of 1900 but it was also a terrifying, tragic era for him as well. He has regrets that life was never so exciting again, but one of the reasons for that was that he was so deeply wounded emotionally that he took steps to protect himself, burying himself in a life of facts rather than coming to terms with the facts of life.

As is often the case in this kind of fiction, innocence is a two-edged sword in *The Go-Between*. It is about innocence destroyed, but also about innocence itself as a destructive force. Innocence does not always mean the same thing in such works (it means something completely different in William Golding's *Lord of the Flies*, for example, when Ralph weeps for 'the end of innocence'), and in *The Go-Between* it should be stressed that innocence means basically the absence of sexual knowledge and awareness. Indeed, in the novel the main way in which Leo's 'child-like' nature is signalled, to distinguish him from the adults, is through his failure to pick up the sexual innuendoes and *double entendres*, which so amuse his elders. If Trimingham is one of the work's most sympathetic characters, the reason is that he is the only adult who treats Leo not like a child but as an equal. By the end of the summer, Leo's innocence has been destroyed: when brought to see Ted and Marian in the act of making love, his own sexual identity is fixed. His frigidity is the result of adult guilt, treachery and hypocrisy, and *The Go-Between* is one of those works that uses children essentially as a means of criticizing the adult world for its exploitation of childish helplessness and ignorance for its own end.

The reverse side of the coin is that, if children become implicated and involved in adult folly without fully understanding it, they may inadvertently bring it down. 'Kids are dangerous – they scare me', says Zac (James Coburn) in *A High Wind in Jamaica*; and *The Go-Between* cannily develops this tradition as well. Leo's trauma stems from his feeling not simply that he was exploited but that he was partly responsible for what happened. For one thing, he continues to be a messenger when he knows the messages are wrong and he knows he is betraying Trimingham. In the novel, in trying to change the last message for his own purposes, he only multiplies the confusion and chaos. In the film, he has already said goodbye to Burgess and it is on impulse that he turns round and offers to take one last message: it is on that single impulse that his whole future will rest. The other element of Leo's guilt is his flirtation with the supernatural and the mysterious effect of his spells and curses. This secret world of children – the odd little codes, rituals, games and hobbies of children – has a particularly poisonous edge to it in *The Go-Between* where Leo's magic injures some schoolboys ('It wasn't a killing curse, you see – there are curses and curses, it depends on the curse . . .'). Finally, it is all part of the apparatus of destruction that will bring an end to the illicit Marian/Burgess liaison (and that *was* a killing curse: 'Die – all evil . . .').

'Seems to be a nice lad', says Mr Maudsley after a first acquaintance with Leo. He is, but he could also be placed in a tradition of childhood that might link him with a character like Pearl in *The Scarlet Letter* (where she seems part precocious child, part witch) or even a very civilized precursor of the demon children of the modern horror film, like *Carrie*, in which children use spells to heap destruction on the heads of erring adults. This would be taking things too far perhaps, but part of the fascination of Leo is the combination in him of likeable shyness and compelling strangeness. Ultimately Hartley's view of childhood seems more Freudian than Wordsworthian and *The Go-Between* becomes an anti-Romantic work. Whereas a film like Boorman's *Hope and Glory*, with its stress on the liberating and purifying effect on its hero of the move from the city to the country, is squarely in the Romantic, Wordsworthian tradition, *The Go-Between* subverts it. Leo will encounter not golden daffodils but deadly nightshades and might have been a lot better off if only he had stayed in the city with his mother.

CHAPTER EIGHT

ARTISTRY AND AUTOBIOGRAPHY

---

*Where is beauty? In nature and in my mood,
when I am kitted out in Sunday best! Where
are faith and honour? In fairy tales and
children's games! Where is that which keeps
its promise? . . . In my imagination!*

(AUGUST STRINDBERG, *The Ghost Sonata*)

*You may not realize it, Sir, but some of our
greatest men started life as children . . . .*

(PETER SELLERS in the Muir-Norden revue sketch
'Common Entrance')

FOR a film director, childhood often turns out to be his first theme or his last. In the case of Charles Laughton with *The Night of the Hunter*, it was both. Film-makers as diverse as Satyajit Ray (*Pather Panchali*, 1955) and Bryan Forbes (*Whistle Down The Wind*, 1961) began their directing careers with films about childhood. The first feature film of François Truffaut (*The 400 Blows*, 1959), Bill Douglas, (*My Childhood*, 1972), and Allen Fong (*Father and Son*, 1981) were recollections of their own childhood on celluloid. Conversely, Ingmar Bergman, with *Fanny and Alexander* in 1982, and Louis Malle, with *Au Revoir, les Enfants* in 1987, saved their definitive films about childhood – more specifically, their own childhood – until late in their careers.

When a director begins his career with a film about his early life, what he is doing is probably heeding the conventional advice of every creative writing tutor: when you start, write about what you know. The only difference is that, whereas many creative artists reach for a pen or typewriter, the modern artist is just as likely to reach for his camera. In telling his story this way, he very often reveals his youthful obsession with

Pather Panchali (1955)

the cinema that explains his career direction. This is what happens in Truffaut's *400 Blows* and Fong's *Father and Son*. But, over and above this, they have another story to tell. Implicit in Truffaut's film is the theme that the cinema saved him from delinquency and even possibly a life of crime: it certainly provided relief from an intolerable home life. Home life figures strongly in Fong's film too, where the young hero's obsession with cinema at first brings him into conflict with his father, who thinks it is no career; and then into conflict with his sisters, who, being the women in the family, have to make sacrifices in order for the son to be able to fulfil his ambition. Bill Douglas's film equally has a remarkable story to tell of a childhood of deprivation and despair, eventually transcended through a love of art and a recognition of kinship with film-makers like Truffaut. What Douglas's film conveys superbly is the nature of a child's world as a series of puzzling visual impressions that only slowly form themselves into a coherent picture. In this way it implies that childhood is a natural theme for cinematic

151

treatment. It also has a wonderful sense of the child as, simultaneously, intruder, outsider and observer: in this respect, it implies the kinship of the child with the artist.

When a mature director such as Woody Allen in *Radio Days*, looks back on his childhood, it is often simply for a pleasurable feeling of nostalgia, revisiting a time that seemed less fraught and hectic, perhaps more romantic. On the other hand, such a journey can be a form of psychoanalysis, an attempt on the part of the artist to unblock a side of his sensibility that seems to have become frozen, as Tarkovsky does in *Mirror*. Alternatively, it can be an attempt to exorcise a particular trauma in the past, as Chaplin rakes over his tormented childhood in *The Kid* or as Louis Malle recalls the fateful day in *Au Revoir, les Enfants* that may well have determined his future. Here the camera is not just a witness but a conscience. In *Fanny and Alexander* one feels that Bergman is returning to his childhood as part of a search for the key to his own personality or artistry, the explanation for whose obsessions are rooted in this early life. Miraculously, in turning his camera back to this time he seems to rediscover a childlike zest for the cinema.

All the following films are by special people telling of their special lives, yet there is a quality of universality about them. They talk about family and about what their parents meant to them. They recall the truism that an artist is not a special kind of person: each person is potentially a special kind of artist. Above all, they suggest the importance to the artist of retaining those

Restricted childhood: Stephen Archibald in Bill Douglas's *My Childhood* (1972)

152

qualities in himself that are most childlike: freshness, fantasy, an openness to new impression and experience. 'The poet', said Coleridge, 'is the one who carries the simplicity of childhood into the powers of manhood, who, with a soul unsubdued by habit, unshackled by custom, contemplates all things with the freshness and wonder of a child.'

THE KID
(USA 1921:Charles Chaplin)

Although *The Kid* was to prove one of Chaplin's greatest and most popular films, one should not forget that, at the time of its making, Chaplin was taking the biggest risk of his professional career. It was the longest film by far of any he had made up to that time, and he had to resist pressure from the distributors to cut the film into three separate parts. More than any other Chaplin or silent film comedy of that time, it was a film full of pathos, with anguish alongside the laughter ('a picture with a smile, and perhaps, a tear ...' says the opening title). Also it was a film with a strong vein of social criticism directed at the way society treats its unfortunates, whether they be an unmarried mother, a tramp, or a kid with no socially sanctioned parents. To court such dangers, Chaplin must have had a deep personal attachment to the project, and although the desire to work with the phenomenally gifted five-year-old Jackie Coogan was the initial spur, the film's intensity undoubtedly comes from its strong autobiographical overtones.

The autobiographical dimension in the film is felt and expressed in several ways. For example, the film was made a year or so after the death of Chaplin's first child, a boy, Norman Spencer, who had lived only three days. It would be difficult to exaggerate the pain the father felt. Strikingly, in his own autobiography, he cannot bring himself even to mention it. Commenting later on their short-lived marriage, Chaplin's first wife said she could really only remember one thing about it: he cried when the baby died. Against this background, *The Kid* can be seen as Chaplin's act of comic catharsis.

Also, in conceiving *The Kid*, Chaplin, more than in any of his previous films, was led to draw on recollections from his own dreadful childhood in Victorian London. The plot concerns a kid who is abandoned by his mother, adopted by the Tramp, taken away by the authorities, rescued by the Tramp, then finally reunited with his mother, who is now successful and also morally rehabilitated through her work with children and for charity. It is an outline with which its creator could readily identify from painful experience: the heart-rending separation from a beloved mother; the horror of being at the mercy of insensitive people who represent authority in society; the fragile sense of family, which alone provides shelter against a hostile world. Even the attic where the Tramp and the kid live was consciously modelled after the attic where Chaplin lived as a boy, and where he remembered that every time he woke up in the morning he would bump his head on the low ceiling.

There is also a submerged personal reference in the similarities *The Kid* shares with Dickens's *Oliver Twist*, throughout his life Chaplin's favourite novel which he read and re-read, undoubtedly because of its similarity and relevance to his own childhood experience. Both begin with the situation of the tragedy of the unmarried mother and the child abandoned to its fate. As it develops, the relationship between the Tramp and the kid becomes a genial variation on Fagin and the Artful Dodger, as the older man teaches his young apprentice the tricks of the trade. Also, although very different in conception and effect, the big set-pieces of both *Oliver Twist* and *The Kid* are roof-top chases – in the former, to trap Bill Sikes, in the latter, to rescue the little boy who has been taken from the Tramp.

It is this separation scene that is the major emotional climax of *The Kid*. Discovering that the Tramp is not the boy's father, the workhouse administrator, supported by the police, comes to take the boy away. The brusqueness of the music and the pomposity of their manner make the film's attitudes clear: these people are acting out of simple officiousness rather than any considered compassion. Moreover, an audience at the time would undoubtedly have recognized that the child, in being sent away to the workhouse, was effectively being sentenced to death. The point is emphasized by the callous way the kid is thrown into the back of the truck, as if he is an animal on the way to the slaughterhouse. The Tramp gives chase across the roof-tops, which is not only a brilliant variation on the *mechanics* of the silent comedy chase (not a mad car chase, but one between a truck and a man on foot across roof-tiles) but also on the *mood* (the accent here is not on slapstick but on suspense). At last he overtakes and jumps into the back of the truck, clasping the boy to him.

At the moment when the Tramp rescues the child, the two actors were both genuinely crying. When the Tramp rescues the boy from death, Chaplin might have been thinking fondly back on his own son: the moment has a poignant feeling of resurrection. But there are other reasons why Chaplin found it an exceptionally emotional scene to direct. He had grown very fond of little Jackie Coogan, for the duration of the film seeing him as a sort of surrogate son; and, rather in the way that Vincente Minnelli dreaded having to induce Margaret O'Brien's hysterics in *Meet Me in St Louis*, he wondered how he could bring him to the necessary point of making him weep wholeheartedly. (Eventually the job was entrusted to Coogan's father who simply told the boy: 'Look, give Mr Chaplin what he wants or you'll get fired, in which case *I'll* send you to the workhouse!') In a later televised interview, the adult Coogan also made a point about the impact on an audience of that time, when Chaplin's sentimentality was not as advanced or as insistent as it would later become. 'To see this great clown, this mischievous tramp, *really* crying', said Coogan, 'was a considerable shock.'

It is typical of Chaplin, nevertheless, that he does not leave the scene there. There is a small comic coda in which the driver of the truck runs away and the Tramp threatens to give chase, in a manner that is very like a kid himself seeing off the street bully. No one could excel Chaplin at the dexterity of his mood changes from comedy to tragedy and then back again, but what is interesting about *The Kid* is the precariousness of this balance between humour and harshness. Comedy might have the upper hand, but there are substantial stretches in the film (the opening before the Tramp appears, the roof-top chase, the Tramp's forlorn search for the kid after he has been kidnapped and returned to his mother for a reward) when humour is almost entirely absent.

Tears of joy: kid (Jackie Coogan) and tramp (*Charlie Chaplin*) reunited in *The Kid* (1921)

Indeed, even in the overtly comic sections, there is invariably a serious undercurrent. When the Tramp first discovers the child dumped on a piece of wasteland, the literal and metaphorical association of them both with garbage is very significant: it is a measure of the way they will be treated. One of the film's main strategies is to demonstrate the enormous gap between the way the authorities and social administrators look on the Tramp and the kid and the warmth of the actual relationship. Similarly when the Tramp and the kid go into business together (the boy breaks windows, along comes the Tramp to mend them, at a cost, for the irate owners), it is hard not to suspect that this is Chaplin's metaphor for the world of business and capitalism generally: a profit-making combination of destruction followed by deception. It is a vision that Chaplin will take to murderous extremes in his masterpiece, *Monsieur Verdoux* (1947).

If the roof-top chase is the film's emotional heart, its most puzzling and controversial section is the Dreamland sequence, which follows the passage when the kid has been kidnapped and the Tramp, exhausted from his unavailing search, flops down in despair and falls asleep in the very spot where the mother has seen her grown child for the first time and has not at that time recognized him. He dreams of Heaven. The simplicity of the imagery (policemen and dogs with wings) must not be confused with absence of visual imagination: it appropriately reflects the simplicity of the Tramp himself and has something of the naïve charm of the child's view of Heaven that concludes Mahler's 4th Symphony. In a nice touch, it is apparent that angelic wings make the Tramp uncomfortable: they itch. It is a scene that prepares for the fairy-tale finale that reunites Tramp and kid and which might also be a dream, and it is a scene that reminds us of the Tramp as a dreamer who, as he will have to so often, can sometimes rise above his appalling situation through sheer will of the imagination. Nevertheless, the dream also includes a vision of 'paradise lost' and the conflict between wish and reality. 'Sin creeps in': the Devil makes his appearance and the Tramp is vamped – incidentally, by a child-actress of the time who, in a few years, was to become Chaplin's second wife. Paradise is fragile and transitory, so the dream says, which must certainly modify our feelings about the film's so-called happy ending.

With *The Kid* Chaplin reached new heights of fame and popularity, but even so at this time he was saying how he could never forget earlier humiliations and poverty and that, at heart, 'I can't feel myself any different from the unhappy and defeated men, the failures'. The dark areas in Chaplin's personality – the egotism, the meanness, the moody insecurity – undoubtedly stem from his childhood experience, just as his survival of that experience gave him the resilience neccessary to withstand the calamities of his later years – the political and moral persecutions by the self-appointed guardians of American values. *The Kid* is the Chaplin film that reaches most deeply and courageously into his childhood, drawing on its anguish for inspiration and transmuting its potential tragedy into permanent art.

MIRROR
(USSR 1975 : Andrei Tarkovsky)

In a prologue to *Mirror*, a boy with a severe speech impediment is hypnotized by a doctor who enjoins him to 'speak loudly and freely, unafraid in your own voice'. Awakening from the trance, the boy begins to speak, clearly and without stuttering.

One is a little reminded of Sergei Rachmaninov who, after the disastrous première of his 1st Symphony had to undergo hypnosis in order to continue as a composer: his ageless 2nd Piano Concerto is dedicated to his hypnotist. Tarkovsky's pre-credit scene (and is this the first pre-credit sequence in Soviet cinema?) seems certainly in part an artistic allegory, an appeal to the artist to express himself openly and personally, and a metaphor for his own artistic situation after what he felt was the stuttering achievement of his previous film, *Solaris* (1972). Tarkovsky's solution to his creative crisis, his means of liberating his artistic personality is to reach back into his childhood to find out who and what he is. In the process, he establishes another first: in Herbert Marshall's words, 'here for the first time is the subjective history of a Soviet film-maker in his own film'.[1]

'Halfway through my earthly life, I lost myself in a gloomy forest.' This is taken from a poem by the director's father, Arsemy Tarkovsky, and is in some ways a springboard for the entire film, as the director finds his way out of the gloomy forest of mid-life crisis through dream, memory, reflections on history, and an interrogation of the character of his parents. The poems of

Tarkovsky Snr – sometimes personal, sometimes political, and infused with compelling natural imagery – are recited by the author at various stages in the film, and are as vital to its atmosphere and intellectual fibre as the poems of the eponymous hero of Boris Pasternak's *Dr Zhivago*. They are a clue to Andrei Tarkovsky's own poetic sensibility, expressed in his case not through words but through cinematic images. When he films a house, or a barn fire, or a child discovering that he is separated from his mother, he films with such freshness that an authentic childlike sensation is created: the feeling that it is being experienced for the first time.

On one level, *Mirror* is an autobiographical film. The narrator (Tarkovsky) looks back to his childhood and particularly the impact on him of the separation of his parents in 1935. In addition to Tarkovsky Snr's poem on the soundtrack, Tarkovsky's mother plays the role of the narrator's mother as an old woman: elsewhere the role of the narrator's mother and of his wife is played by the same actress, Margarita Terekhova, who plays the former role with her hair up and the latter with her hair down. It is in a way Tarkovsky's $8\frac{1}{2}$ and also his equivalent to Bergman's *Persona*, an exorcizing of ghosts in the director's psyche and an extraordinarily imaginative use of a fractured dramatic form to suggest a psychology under pressure.

Mirror is partially a study of character and how certain features in a personality can mirror those of his or her parents. It is also about memory – of the people and places of one's childhood – and about dreams and images that serve as metaphors for an actual situation: a fire, spilt milk, objects being blown off a table, enlarge the theme of family instability and of the security of a family home being battered by storms.

Inevitably, it is also about growing up at a particular time in history, where one's childhood memories are especially bound up in war. However, whereas Tarkovsky's first film *Ivan's Childhood* was a more objective biography of a young Russian boy in the Second World War, *Mirror* is more immediately personal and relates to the situation of a child growing up under the shadow of Stalin. Tarkovsky expands this theme in one enigmatic, extended episode where the narrator's mother rushes back in panic through a storm to her printing works to double-check the proofs she had been correcting the previous day. The mistake is discovered, and there is a huge sigh of relief: it is a telling cameo of the prevailing atmosphere of fear. The incident, apparently, was inspired by a famous occasion when a typographical error in *Pravda* converted the name of 'Stalin' to 'Sralin' – which, literally translated, means 'the man of shit'. Everyone involved with the error was arrested.

The use of historical newsreel within the structure of the film is also significant as part of the fabric that has formed the narrator's (i.e. the director's) personality. There is some propaganda film of the record breaking ascent of a Soviet balloon, the kind of event traditionally celebrated by the media to emphasize national pride; but there is also extensive footage of the Red Army as it crosses Lake Sivash during the Soviet advance of 1943 – people dragging themselves through an endless swamp, a distillation of war as mud and drudgery and of what Tarkovsky called 'that suffering which is the price of what is known as historical progress'.[2] Also evocatively quoted are newsreel pictures of children being separated from their parents during the Spanish Civil War, which parallel the separation of the narrator's parents but give it a larger, more tragic historical dimension. There is also a leap forward to the Maoist China of 1969, where the cult of personality being so assiduously pursued mirrors the kind of Stalinist society in which the narrator grew up.

Because it weaves so freely between past and present, colour and black-and-white, dream and memory, dramatized reality and historical newsreel, *Mirror* is an inordinately difficult film to do justice to in words. Films should be experienced, not explained, thought Tarkovsky, and no film-maker surpassed him in being able, as it were, to film the human spirit. The fact that it had such an impact on the intelligentsia and ordinary people in the Soviet Union suggests that it transcends esoteric personal reference and touches something universal in us all. Yet it does also seem a film that offers a kind of key to Tarkovsky's artistic personality, and to his other films: where, for example, his sensitivity to nature comes from; his portrayal of disappointed women; his particular anxiety over war and conflict; and even recurrent images in his films like spilt milk, or the drawings of Leonardo (here the portrait 'A Young Lady With a Jumper' reminds him of his mother). All have their origins, *Mirror* suggests, in his childhood. It is this remembrance of things past, this desire to understand and pay off the debt he feels to those people who gave him life, that unfreezes his creative block and produces the unique artistic structure that is *Mirror* – a kind of confession, and a kind of exorcism. After it, Tarkovsky said, 'childhood memories which for years had given me no peace suddenly vanished, as if they had melted away, and at last I stopped dreaming about the house where I had lived so many years before. . . .'[3]

FANNY AND ALEXANDER
(Sweden 1982:Ingmar Bergman)

Like Thomas Hardy, Ingmar Bergman nearly died at birth: does that in any way provide a key to their gloomy artistic temperaments? Fellow Swedish film-maker Kjell Gede, who is best known for his lovely film about childhood, *Hugo and Josefin* (1970), put the question another way. Why do you make such gloomy films, he asked Bergman gently one day, when you yourself so obviously relish life and often find it amusing? The remark set Bergman's imagination racing and the eventual result was *Fanny and Alexander*, his most life-affirming film and also his most autobiographical, with the material being full of recollections of his childhood.

Yet the literal events connected with Bergman's own childhood have been transformed by imagination, which is highly appropriate: the transforming power of imagination, which can sometimes transcend reality, is one of the film's key themes. The setting is the university town of Uppsala in 1907, roughly the time and the place when Bergman himself was growing up as a boy. Like the young Bergman, Alexander's most pleasurable times are at his grandmother's and his most treasured plaything is his first toy film projector. Like the young Bergman also, Alexander finds himself as a young boy having to endure the iron discipline of the family, the volatile moods of a religious father, beatings and incarcerations that are incurred when his flights of imagination are interpreted as lies. Bergman's drama is by no

158

Conflict between
Alexander (Berlin Guve,
centre) and the bishop
(Jan Malmsjö, left) in
Fanny and Alexander
(1982): Fanny (Pernilla
Allwin) watches
anxiously

means strictly autobiographical recollection, however. He has said that he
recognizes himself less in the young Alexander than in the evil bishop,
grappling with his own personal demons. Also Alexander's principal
antagonist, unlike the young Bergman's, is not his father but his new
stepfather. As well as being inspired by Bergman's own early life, *Fanny and
Alexander* also owes much of its inspiration to *Hamlet*.

Like *Hamlet*, *Fanny and Alexander* divides into five acts. Act One
introduces the prosperous theatrical family of the Ekdahls, to which young
Alexander (Bertil Guve) and his younger sister, Fanny (Pernilla Allwin),
belong, as they all gather for the traditional family celebration of Christmas
at the home of Fanny and Alexander's grandmother (Gunn Wållgren). The
dominant events of Acts Two and Three are the death of their father, Oscar
(Allan Edwall), and the remarriage of their mother, Emilie (Ewa Fröling), to
sinister Bishop Edvard Vergerus (Jan Malmsjöe). In Act Four the antagonism
between Alexander and the bishop intensifies to the point where Alexander
is whipped, and mother and children become effectively prisoners in the
bishop's house. However, the final act sees the children magically spirited

out of Vergerus's house in a chest by their grandmother's close friend, the antique dealer Isak Jacobi (Erland Josephson); the escape of their mother, and the accidental burning to death of the bishop; and a family reunion, which celebrates the birth to Emilie of a new baby girl, and the contemplation by both Emilie and grandmother of a return to the stage. At the close, grandmother is seen reading from *A Dream Play*, by the dramatist who has been Bergman's biggest artistic influence, August Strindberg: 'Anything can happen, everything is possible and plausible. Time and space do not exist. Against an insignificant background, the imagination spins and weaves new designs.'

If *Fanny and Alexander* seems Bergman's freshest and most playful film for years, much of this has undoubtedly to do with the fact that he makes a conscious attempt to reflect reality from a child's point of view. He recognizes that this is different from that of an adult and therefore requires a different kind of style from that with which an adult audience would be familiar. He therefore employs a judicious mixture of stylization and the grotesque. Everything is heightened to reflect the intensity and newness of a child's vision. Grandmother's home seems more like a brilliantly lit theatre, whilst Jacobi's antique shop is an Aladdin's cave of mystery and fantasy. The colour is equally starkly contrasted: rich and luxurious for the Ekdahl home, pallid and almost monochrome for the bishop's home; the ghost of Alexander's father appears always in white whilst the bishop is seen always in black, as Alexander sees them as Good and Evil, respectively. Emilie is an idealization of maternal beauty, whereas someone like the bishop's servant Justina (Harriet Anderson) becomes the epitome of servile treachery.

Rising to the challenge of a child's-eye view, Bergman has fashioned a tale that is almost a Dickensian fairy-tale – full of ghosts and ogres, fantasy and suspense. Like *Hamlet*, it features the ghost of a dead father, jealousy between son and stepfather over the love of the mother, a setting that becomes like a prison. But it also has some magical sleights of hand, like the moment when the bishop devilishly conjures up the spirit of Emilie to convince the visiting Ekdahls of her happiness, or the whole episode where Jacobi sneaks the children away from their prison under the very nose of their jailers. It is Bergman's own magic lantern show, with familiar themes – the tensions between art and life, religious doubt and bigotry – given a fresh glow that comes partly from the serenity of age and partly from a great artist's capacity for wonder at life's variety.

For a film entitled *Fanny and Alexander*, it might seem that Fanny does not have much of a look-in and, in contrast to her dynamic brother, is as passive in the face of religious evil as young Pearl is in *The Night of the Hunter*. This is slightly deceptive, however. Fanny seems more dumpily down-to-earth than her brooding brother, and in some ways more of a survivor. Indeed, it is striking that the women in the film endure, even under duress, whereas the men decline or die; and that the births that conclude the film are all of girls. Symbolically, it represents the downfall of the age of patriarchal control, and a new age in which women will be more assertive and better able to discover their full potential. Of the forthcoming film artists who will play tribute to the more liberated women of our modern century, no one will do it better than Ingmar Bergman. Fanny, even more than Alexander, is the future.

RADIO DAYS
(USA 1987: Woody Allen)

Woody Allen's own description of *Radio Days* is probably the most accurate definition of its elusive genre and charm: 'It's a nostalgic comedy without a plot, just sort of a part documentary, part plot account of certain years of my childhood, unrelated little incidents that I happen to know about either secondhand, or that I remember firsthand.' It is a reconstruction of the period from 1938 until 1944, told partly through the radio programmes (mostly invented by Woody Allen) broadcast during the period, and partly through the unseen narrator's memory of his own boyhood. It is an account of an upbringing in Rockaway, Brooklyn, as little Joey (Seth Green) remembers his times at school – the games with the snowman, his friends, his crush on the teacher, his first interest in girls – but whose memories are mainly preoccupied with his family and his fantasies.

His family includes Mum (Julie Kavner), who keeps a tight rein on the household ('I like to daydream, but I have my two feet planted firmly on my husband'); Dad (Michael Tucker), a dreamer who keeps his job a secret from his son (the excitement is rather deflated when the boy discovers his dad is merely a cab driver); and Aunt Bea (Dianne Wiest), a single lady singularly

Happy family: Julie Kavner, Seth Green and Michael Tucker in *Radio Days* (1987)

unfortunate in her choice of men, never more so than when she is left stranded in the fog by one of her beaux who has inadvertently tuned in to Orson Welles's Martian broadcast and fled in terror. As in George Stevens's *Penny Serenade* (1941) or, more recently, Terence Davies's *Distant Voices, Still Lives* (1988), song serves as a trigger for the narrator's memory. 'Paper Doll', for example, reminds him of his parents' anniversary because it was the only time that he saw them kiss. Sometimes he imagines his parents' participation in some of his favourite radio programmes, as in a fantasy where they appear in a programme devoted to people's problems. 'I love him,' says Mum of Dad, 'but what did I do to deserve him?'

As vivid as the memory of his family is the memory of his great hero on radio, the Masked Avenger. The young boy imagines him to be a dashingly handsome mixture of Superman and Cary Grant: he is actually played by Woody Allen's favourite embodiment of romantic let-down, Wallace Shawn (he played a similar role in *Manhattan*). Of course in radio, you do not have to look the part. 'Now basically I was an honest kid', says Joey, 'but there are some things in life that are too compelling', referring to the Masked Avenger Secret Compartment Ring. Joey cannot afford it but sets about raising the money by going round with a collection box for a Jewish homeland. When reprimanded by his Rabbi (Kenneth Mars) for his dishonesty, Joey says solemnly, 'You speak the truth, my faithful Indian companion', and is clipped across the head for his cheek.

The narrator supplements his own story with other choice anecdotes: the story of two burglars who win the jackpot on the 'Guess that Tune' phone-in radio programme, forgetting that the phone they are using is not their own; the story of the match-girl (Mia Farrow) who becomes a gossip-columnist, after nearly being the victim of a Mafia hit and whose radio acting career has been interrupted by world events ('Who is Pearl Harbor?' she demands, indignantly); the story of an eventually limbless baseball player who nevertheless 'had *heart*'. All of the stories play in the space between fantasy and reality, dream and disillusionment. None is more powerful than that moment when a family row is interrupted by a live report on the radio about a little girl who has fallen down a well and the rescue mission to save her. A family and nation momentarily shed their differences to tune in and root for a child in peril, but when the girl is brought to the surface she is dead. Life, and even the media, cannot always contrive a happy ending, and the lesson is to value what one has. Dad, who has previously been chasing Joey round the house to punish him for some indiscretion, now finds himself weeping on his shoulder.

'Now it's all gone except for the memories . . .' says the narrator. 'Forgive me if I romanticize the past.' Although the film is not as autobiographical as some of Woody Allen's other films, such as *Annie Hall* (1977) or *Stardust Memories* (1980), it still has things in it that are clearly very personal and do give an insight into the mature Woody Allen and the derivation of some of his themes and techniques: the fascination with family, the split between dream and reality, the evocative and expressive use of music from the big band era. It reminds one of Woody's portrayal of the child in some of his earlier films, such as *Love and Death* (1975) and *Annie Hall*, where, in bespectacled bemusement, he is already fretful about the problems of existence. In *Radio Days*, the child is an observer more than a participator, not so much an initiator of events as a cataloguer of incidents, for whom the inimitable heyday of radio – on which even a ventriloquist could be a star comedian – serves as the most valuable catalyst for memory.

AU REVOIR, LES ENFANTS

(France 1987 : Louis Malle)

Louis Malle's most anarchic film about childhood is *Zazie dans le Métro* (1960). Catherine Demengeot (centre) played Zazie; Philippe Noiret (left) her uncle

From the anarchic antics of his young heroine in *Zazie dans le Métro* (1960) to the controversial study of child prostitution in *Pretty Baby* (1978), the films of Louis Malle have often been preoccupied with children and particularly their sudden confrontation with moral dilemmas of a complexity beyond their years. Prematurely, the child is compelled to ponder why adults lie and why the world is nonsense. It was predictable that Malle would one day be tempted to make a film about an aspect of his own childhood and *Au Revoir, les Enfants* is that film. He has said that it might well have been the subject of his first film – the closing shot of his young hero is a sort of homage to the

famous ending of the début feature of his Nouvelle Vague colleague, François Truffauts's *Les Quatre Cents Coups* – but he hesitated and allowed the years to refine his filmic technique and sharpen his memories and imagination. The focus is a fateful morning in 1944, when Malle was 11 and his world was turned savagely upside down.

The boy who represents Malle in the film is Julien, superbly played by Gaspard Manesse. We first meet him on a railway platform as he is saying farewell to his mother (Francine Racette) and preparing to board the train that will return him to his Catholic boarding school. Malle is not overly kind to himself at this point. Julien is moody and petulant about having to return, clearly a bit of a mother's boy, and revealing an immature, somewhat spoilt sensitivity. 'Do you think I like it?' his mother says, cajolingly, 'I'd like to dress up as a boy and come out with you.' It is a mischievous, slightly ridiculous joke, but, in retrospect, it hints at what is to be an important theme of the film: that of disguise. In retrospect also, this farewell scene will contrast painfully with the film's ending, which will be a farewell that is genuinely final and death-haunted and will be the moment when Julien grows up.

The scenes at school seem initially in a familiar vein of French cinema, from Jean Vigo's 1932 classic, *Zero de Conduite* (anarchy and revelry in the dormitory), to the violent playgrounds of Truffaut. There is even a fleeting similarity to Boorman's *Hope and Glory* in the relief with which an air-raid is greeted as an interruption of a boring lesson. The imagery – mock jousts on stilts in an icy playground – catches something of every school's air of surrealism, which Bill Forsyth also caught in *Gregory's Girl* (1981). Overall it has something of the aura of Alain-Fournier's *Le Grand Meaulnes*, and Jean Cocteau's novel *Les Enfants Terribles*: like them, it is also about an adolescence abbreviated by death and about an idealized friend whose memory smites your heart. What is remarkable about the film is the way it draws on tradition and yet is simultaneously wholly individual and original. This feeling of freshness and surprise derives partly from the skill of its structure. Every scene, almost every detail, has a deeper significance when seen in the light of the devastating denouement.

It would take too long to demonstrate this exhaustively, but some examples will suffice. In an early scene, it is casually revealed that Julien is reading *The Memoirs of Sherlock Holmes*. It is an anticipation of the detective work he will later pursue, in the process discovering that a class newcomer, Bonnet (an excellent performance by Raphael Fejto), who was at first a resented scholastic rival but has become his best friend, is actually a Jew called Kippelstein who is being hidden by the priest from the Gestapo. In connection with this, one might also remember a small moment when Julien is discovered pricking himself with a compass and drawing blood. His experiment with pain-endurance will seem childish in the extreme by the end in comparison with the pain his friend will be marched off to face. (Similarly, Julien's agony at his bed-wetting, or Bonnet's persecution by his school-fellows will fall into diminished perspective in context of the horror that is to befall the school.) Indeed, this image of the compass causes a quick reminiscence of the Jew Shylock's famous speech in *The Merchant of Venice* as he insists on his common humanity: 'If you prick me, do I not bleed . . .'

164

Boyhood friends to be violently parted: Bonnet (Raphael Fejto) and Julien (Gaspard Manesse) in *Au Revoir, les Enfants* (1987)

'You're a real Jew,' Julien is told when driving a hard bargain for his stamps with the kitchen boy, Joseph (François Negret), who is the school's black marketeer. It is a comment that seems an unwitting premonition of Julien's forthcoming friendship with Bonnet as well as a phrase that carries the kind of casual racism that can so often be inflamed into persecution. The character of Joseph is the twin of the leading character whom Malle explored in his previous film of collaboration and betrayal in wartime France, *Lacombe Lucien* (1974). In both characters Malle attempts to discover the appeal of Fascism for the underprivileged, and offers the following phrase as explanation: it is 'the revenge of the humiliated'. Joseph is an orphan who is treated with contempt by the boys but who, when the black marketeering in the school is discovered, is the one who is singled out for punishment and dismissed, despite being no more guilty than the rich boys with whom he has traded. A crippled outsider, Joseph turns collaborator through a combination of abuse, mockery and, finally, unjust victimization. He tips off the Nazis about Jews being hidden at the school.

The Nazi threat has been growing in prominence through the film – a soldier glimpsed through a school window, then a straggling collection of militia relaxing in the swimming baths. Two incidents play with this threat in an ironically suspenseful way. When Julien and Bonnet are lost in a wood during a scouting exercise, they think the monster they have to fear is a prowling wild boar: they are quite unprepared for something even more frightening, which is being picked up by some German soldiers on the road. Yet the Germans are friendly, plead kinship ('We Bavarians are Catholics too') and deposit the boys safely back at school. Equally tense and ironic is a marvellous scene at a restaurant where Bonnet is dining with Julien's family and has to witness an elderly Jew being harassed by French soldiers who are helping the Nazi occupation. Partly out of exasperation at the interruption of his meal but also probably to impress Julien's attractive mother, a Nazi soldier orders the officious Frenchmen out of the restaurant, and the danger is averted. It is a measure of Malle's complex and uncomfortable sense of human nature that he can characterize the behaviour of a Nazi in this way, but it is also indicative of his dramatic cunning in keeping an audience on edge. Bonnet has survived two close encounters with the Nazis, but how much longer can this charmed life last?

In a scene that follows, there is another example of Malle's gift at intensifying the tension even as he seems to be relieving it. The boys and the priest watch Charlie Chaplin in his famous short *The Immigrant* (1916) and Malle quotes what is surely the most extraordinary single image in Chaplin's work (also quoted in Terrence Malick's *Days of Heaven* in a very different context): the moment when the immigrants sail past the Statue of Liberty but, before having the chance even to savour their excitement, are roped together by the ship's crew. The yearning for liberty is as strong in that French audience of 1944 as it was in Chaplin's time, but the brutal herding together of the immigrants like cattle is a shivering premonition of concentration camps.

'Do you realize that there'll never be another January 17th 1944?' says Julien as he is walking into school. 'Never ever? I'm the only one who thinks about death at the college.' It is one of those pompous, philosophical flourishes to which the over-serious Julien is prone. Yet in this case, and in a terrible sense, he will be proved right. There never will be another day like this one, a day when his youth ends and his growing love for Bonnet is blown asunder. The long final sequence of that fateful morning, when the Nazis burst into the school in search of the Jewish children the priests have been harbouring, is one of the great sequences of modern cinema. The fear is palpable; everyone seems capable of betrayal or of being betrayed; and in being forced to drop his trousers as the Nazis check for evidence of circumcision, the previously pampered Julien is suddenly tasting the humiliation of the persecuted. Malle is unrivalled in being able to convey menace without, as it were, raising his voice. There is little actual violence, but the atmosphere is terrifying, and the German commander has a quiet arrogance that chills the blood. He is looking, he tells the class, for a boy by the name of 'Kippelstein'. Fatally, Julien darts a look of apprehension at his friend; in that split second, the Nazi intercepts the look; and the fate of Bonnet is sealed. It is a sign of the times that a look, instigated by friendship and concern, is also one that can sentence someone to death. Malle has, he has said, been haunted all his life by that moment in the classroom, when he might unwittingly have revealed his friend's secret. Is it any wonder that, if

166

First encounter with the world of film in *Cinema Paradiso* (1988)

there is a single theme to which Malle has obsessively returned in his work, it is the theme of betrayal?

Herded out on to the playground, the boys must watch as the Jews and the priests who protected them are marched off to concentration camps – never, we are told, to return. 'Au revoir, les enfants', calls out Father Jean to the boys. Bonnet turns to look back at his friend and Julien, in tears of new recognition and rage at the depths and dimensions of adult wickedness, gives a brief wave as the camera lingers on his stricken face. It is a pledge that Bonnet/Kippelstein and the actual boy from Malle's past will not be forgotten; and a reconstruction of the single moment in his life, Malle has said, that might well have determined his vocation as a film-maker. Nothing could make a finer and more fitting ending to this book: a moment that simultaneously signals the end of childhood and the beginning of cinema.

FILMOGRAPHY

This filmography lists the movies about childhood that have been discussed in this book, plus half-a-dozen recent movies on the same theme, which have appeared since the book was completed. These comprise: two major art movies (*Landscape in the Mist, Toto the Hero*), an offbeat character study (*Celia*), the directorial début of Jodie Foster (*Little Man Tate*), a hymn to the shaping force of cinema on childish imagination (*Cinema Paradiso*) and a kids' movie that has rapidly become the most popular film comedy in the history of the cinema (*Home Alone*). These recent films alone underline the continuing variety and vitality of the childhood theme in films. Even as I write, I am turning over in my head the experience of Steven Spielberg's long-awaited revisionist version of *Peter Pan, Hook* (1991) where Neverland has become Disneyworld, where the Lost Boys have become more like the Bad News Bears, but where paradoxically, Spielberg's film seems less full of childish wonder than of paternal anxiety. Films about childhood will continue to proliferate, and be revealing of their makers' personalities and their societies' state of civilization: no theme is more stimulating to the imagination nor more universal in appeal. 'Any life is interesting and always strange', said T. S. Eliot; this is doubly true of everyone's childhood.

Key to abbreviations: *art dir* = artistic director; *dir* = director; *ed* = editor; *LP* = leading players; *m* = music; *phot* = photography; *prod* = producer; *scr* = script.

Children at play in
Whistle Down the Wind

Angels with Dirty Faces (USA 1938: 97 mins).
Warner *dir* Michael Curtiz *prod* Sam Bischoff *scr* John Wexley, Warren Duff, from a story by Rowland Brown *phot* Sol Polito *art dir* Robert Haas *ed* Owen Marks *m* Max Steiner. *LP*: James Cagney, Pat O'Brien, Humphrey Bogart, Ann Sheridan, George Bancroft, the 'Dead End' kids (Bobby Halop, Gabriel Dell, Leo Gorcey, Bobby Jordan, Huntz Hall, Bernard Punsley, Joe Downing).

Au Revoir, les Enfants (France 1987: 103 mins).
Nouvelle Editions De Films *dir, prod, scr* Louis Malle *phot* Renato Berta *art dir* Willy Holt *ed* Emmanuelle Castro *m* Schubert, Saint-Saens. *LP*: Gaspard Manesse, Raphael Fejto, Francine Racette, Philippe Morier-Genoud, Francois Negret.

The Bad News Bears (USA 1976: 102 mins).
Paramount *dir* Michael Ritchie *prod* Stanley R. Jaffe *scr* Bill Lancaster *phot* John Alonzo *art dir* Polly Platt *ed* Richard A. Harris *m* Jerry Fielding, Bizet. *LP*: Walter Matthau, Tatum O'Neal, Vic Morrow.

The Black Stallion (USA 1979: 118 mins).
United Artists *dir* Carroll Ballard *prod* Fred Roos, Tom Sternberg *scr* Melissa Mathison, Jeanne Rosenberg, William D. Wittliff, from the novel by Walter Farley *phot* Caleb Deschanel *art dir* Aurelio Crugnola, Earl Preston *ed* Robert Dalva *m* Carmine Coppola. *LP*: Kelly Reno, Mickey Rooney, Teri Garr, Hoyt Axton, Clarence Muse, Michael Higgins.

Bicycle Thieves (Italy 1948: 90 mins).
Un Film POS (produzione de Sica) *dir* Vittorio de Sica *prod* Umberto Scarpelli *scr* Cesare Zavattini, from the novel by Luigi Bartolini *phot* Carlo Montuori *m* Alessandro Cicognini. *LP*: Lamberto Maggiorani, Enzo Staiola, Lianella Carell.

Celia (Australia 1988: 103 mins).
Seon Film Productions *dir* Ann Turner *prod* Timothy White, Gordon Glenn *scr* Ann Turner *phot* Geoffrey Simpson *art dir* Peta Lawson *ed* Ken Sallows *m* Chris Neal. *LP*: Rebecca Smart, Nicholas Ede, Mary-Ann Fahey, Margaret Rickets, Victoria Longley, Alexander Hutchinson, Martin Sharman, Adrian Mitchell, William Zappa.

Cinema Paradiso (Italy 1988: 123 mins).
Cristaldifilm/Films Ariane *dir* Giuseppe Tornatore *prod* Franco Cristaldi *scr* Giuseppe Tornatore *phot* Blasco Giurato *art dir* Andrea Crisanti *ed* Mario Morra *m* Ennio Morricone. *LP*: Philippe Noiret, Jacques Perrin, Salvator Cascio.

Citizen Kane (USA 1941: 119 mins).
RKO Radio Pictures *dir, prod* Orson Welles *scr* Herman J. Mankiewicz, Orson Welles *phot* Greg Toland *art dir* Van Nest Polglase *ed* Robert Wise, Mark Robson *m* Bernard Herrmann. *LP*: Orson Welles, Joseph Cotten, Agnes Moorehead, George Coulouris, Dorothy Comingore, Everett Sloane, Ray Collins, Ruth Warwick, Paul Stewart, William Alland, Fortunio Bonanova.

The Curse of the Cat People (USA 1944: 70 mins).
RKO *dir* Robert Wise, Gunther von Fritsch *prod* Val Lewton *scr* De Witt Bodeen *phot* Nicholas Musuraca *art dir* Albert S. D'Agostina, Walter E. Keller *ed* J. R. Whittredge *m* Roy Webb. *LP*: Simone Simon, Ann Carter, Kent Smith, Jane Randolph, Julia Dean, Elizabeth Russell, Sir Lancelot.

Days of Heaven (USA 1978: 95 mins).
Paramount *dir* Terrence Malick *prod* Bert Schneider, Harold Schneider *scr* Terrence Malick *phot* Nestor Almendros, Heskell Wexler *art dir* Jack Fisk *ed* Billy Weber *m* Ennio Morricone, Saint-Saens. *LP*: Richard Gere, Brooke Adams, Sam Shepard, Linda Manz, Robert Wilke.

Dead End (USA 1937: 90 mins).
Goldwyn/United Artists *dir* William
Wyler *prod* Sam Goldwyn *scr* Lillian
Hellman, from the play by Sidney
Kingsley *phot* Greg Toland *art dir* Richard
Day *ed* Daniel Mandell *m* Alfred Newman.
LP: Sylvia Sidney, Joel McCrae,
Humphrey Bogart, Marjorie Main, Claire
Trevor, the 'Dead End' kids.

Empire of the Sun (USA 1987: 152 mins).
Amblin/Warner *dir* Steven Spielberg *prod*
Steven Spielberg, Kathleen Kennedy,
Frank Marshall *scr* Tom Stoppard, from
the novel by J. G. Ballard *phot* Allen
Daviau *art dir* Norman Reynolds *ed*
Michael Kahn *m* John Williams. *LP*:
Christian Bale, John Malkovich, Miranda
Richardson, Nigel Havers, Joe Pantoliano.

L'Enfant Sauvage (France 1969: 84 mins).
Les Films du Carosse *dir, prod* François
Truffaut *scr* François Truffaut, Jean
Grualt, from *Memoire et Rapport sur Victor
De L'Aveyron* by Jean Itard *phot* Agnes
Guillemot *m* Vivaldi. *LP*: François
Truffaut, Jean-Pierre Cargol, Jean Daste,
François Seigner.

E.T. – The Extra-Terrestrial (USA 1982:
115 mins).
Universal *dir, prod* Steven Spielberg *scr*
Melissa Mathison *phot* Allen Daviau *art dir*
James D. Bissell *ed* Carol Littleton *m* John
Williams. *LP*: Henry Thomas, Dee
Wallace, Peter Coyote, Robert
McNaughton, Drew Barrymore.

The Exorcist (USA 1973: 121 mins).
Warner *dir* William Friedkin *prod, scr*
William Petty Blatty, based on his novel
phot Owen Roizman, Billy Williams *art dir*
Bill Malley *ed* Jordan Leondopoulos, Evan
Lottman, Norman Gay, Bud Smith *m* Jack
Nitzsche. *LP*: Linda Blair, Ellen Burstyn,
Max von Sydow, Lee J. Cobb, Jack
McGowran, Jason Miller.

The Fallen Idol (GB 1948: 94 mins).
London Films *dir, prod* Carol Reed *scr*
Graham Greene, from his short story 'The
Basement Room' *phot* Georges Perinal *art
dir* Vincent Korda *ed* Oswald Hafenrichter
m William Alwyn. *LP*: Ralph Richardson,
Michele Morgan, Bobby Henrey, Sonia
Dresdel, Jack Hawkins, Dora Bryan.

Fanny and Alexander (Sweden 1983: 188
mins).
Svenska Filminstitutet *dir, prod, scr*
Ingmar Bergman *phot* Sven Nykvist *art dir*
Anna Asp *ed* Sylvia Ingemarsson *m* Daniel
Bell, Britten, Schumann. *LP*: Bertil Guve,
Gunn Wallgren, Ewa Fröling, Jarl Kulle,
Erland Josephson, Harriet Andersson,
Allan Edwall, Jan Malmsjo.

The 5,000 Fingers of Dr T (USA 1953: 89
mins).
Columbia *dir* Roy Rowland *prod* Stanley
Kramer *scr* Dr Seuss (Ted Geisel), Allan
Scott *phot* Franz Planer *art dir* Rudolph
Sternad *ed* Al Clark *m* Frederick Hollander.
LP: Tommy Rettig, Hans Conried, Peter
Lind Hayes, Mary Healey.

Forbidden Games: Jeux Interdits
(France 1952: 102 mins).
Silver Films *dir* René Clément *prod* Robert
Dorfmann *scr* Jean Aurenche, Pierre Bost,
René Clément, Françoise Boyer, from the
novel by Françoise Boyer *art dir* Paul
Bertrand *m* Narciso Yepes. *LP*: Brigitte
Fossey, Georges Poujouly.

**The Four Hundred Blows: Les Quatre
Cents Coups** (France 1959: 94 mins).
Les Films du Carosse *dir, prod, scr* François
Truffaut *phot* Henri Decae *art dir* Bernard
Evein *ed* Marie-Josephe Yoyotte *m* Jean
Constantin. *LP*: Jean-Pierre Léaud, Claude
Maurier, Albert Remy, Jeanne Moreau,
Jean-Claude Brialy.

The Go-Between (GB 1970: 116 mins).
EMI/World Film Services *dir* Joseph Losey
prod John Heyman, Norman Priggen *scr*
Harold Pinter, from the novel by L. P.
Hartley *phot* Gerry Fisher *art dir* Carmen
Dillon *ed* Reginald Beck *m* Michel Legrand.
LP: Julie Christie, Alan Bates, Dominic
Guard, Edward Fox, Margaret Leighton,
Michael Gough, Michael Redgrave.

A High Wind in Jamaica (GB 1965: 103
mins).
20th Century Fox *dir* Alexander
Mackendrick *prod* John Croydon *scr*
Stanley Mann, Ronald Harwood, Denis
Cannan, from the novel by Richard
Hughes *phot* Douglas Slocombe *art dir*
John Hoesli *ed* Derek York *m* Larry Adler.
LP: Anthony Quinn, James Coburn, Lila
Kedrova, Deborah Baxter, Martin Amis,
Dennis Price, Nigel Davenport, Gert Frobe,
Isabel Dean.

Home Alone (USA 1990: 103 mins).
20th Century Fox *dir* Chris Columbus *prod,
scr* John Hughes *phot* Julio Macat *art dir*
John Muto, Dan Webster *ed* Raja Gosnell
m John Williams. *LP*: Macauley Culkin,
Joe Pesci, Daniel Stern, John Heard,
Catherine O'Hara, Roberts Blossom, John
Candy.

Hope and Glory (GB 1987: 113 mins).
Columbia *dir, prod, scr* John Boorman *phot*
Philippe Rousselot *art dir* Anthony Pratt
ed Ian Crafford *m* Peter Martin. *LP*:
Sebastian Rice-Edwards, Geraldine Muir,
Sarah Miles, David Hayman, Derrick
O'Connor, Susan Woolridge, Sammi Davis,
Ian Bannen.

Hue and Cry (GB 1947: 82 mins).
Ealing *dir* Charles Crichton *prod* Henry
Cornelius *scr* T. E. B. Clarke *phot* Douglas
Slocombe *art dir* Norman Arnold *ed*
Charles Hasse *m* Georges Auric. *LP*:
Alistair Sim, Jack Warner, Harry Fowler.

The Innocents (GB 1961: 99 mins).
20th Century Fox *dir, prod* Jack Clayton
scr William Archibald, Truman Capote,
from the novel *The Turn of the Screw* by
Henry James *phot* Freddic Francis *art dir*
Wilfred Shingleton *ed* James Clark *m*
Georges Auric. *LP*: Deborah Kerr, Martin
Stephens, Pamela Franklin, Megs Jenkins,
Peter Wyngarde, Michael Redgrave.

Ivan's Childhood (USSR 1962: 95 mins).
Mosfilm *dir* Andrei Tarkovsky *scr*
Vladimir Bogomolov, Michael Papava,
from the story 'Ivan' by Vladimir
Bogomolov *phot* Vadim Yusov *art dir* V.
Chernyaev *m* Vyacheslav Ovchinnikov.
LP: Kolya Burlyaev, I. Tarkovskaya,
Valentin Zubkov.

Kes (GB 1969: 109 mins).
Woodfall *dir* Ken Loach *prod* Tony Garnett
scr Barry Hines, Ken Loach, Tony Garnett,
from the novel *A Kestrel for a Knave* by
Barry Hines *phot* Chris Menges *art dir*
William McCrow *ed* Roy Watts *m* John
Cameron. *LP*: David Bradley, Freddie
Fletcher, Colin Welland, Brian Glover,
Lynne Perrie.

The Kid (USA 1921: 60 mins).
First National *dir, prod, scr* Charles Chaplin
phot Roland Totheroh *art dir* Charles D.
Hall *ed, m* Charles Chaplin. *LP*: Charles
Chaplin, Jackie Coogan, Edna Purviance,
Lillita McMurray (Lita Grey).

Landscape in the Mist
(Greece/France/Italy 1988: 124 mins).
Artificial Eye *dir prod*, Theo Angelopoulos
scr Theo Angelopoulos, Tonino Guerra,
Thannis Valtinos *phot* Giorgos Arvanitis
art dir Mikes Karapiperis *ed* Yannis
Tsitsopoulos *m* Eleni Karaindrou. *LP*:
Michalis Zeke, Tania Palaiologou, Stratos
Tzortzoglou.

Little Man Tate (USA 1991: 99 mins).
Orion *dir* Jodie Foster *prod* Scott Rudin,
Peggy Rajshi *scr* Scott Frank *phot* Mike
Southon *art dir* John Hutman, Adam
Lustig *ed* Lynzee Klingman *m* Mark Isham.
LP: Jodie Foster, Dianne Wiest, Adam
Hann-Byrd.

Mandy (US title: *The Crash of Silence*) (GB
1952: 93 mins).
Ealing *dir* Alexander Mackendrick *prod*
Leslie Norman *scr* Nigel Balchin, Jack
Whittingham, from the novel *The Day is*

Ours by Hilda Lewis *phot* Douglas Slocombe *art dir* Jim Morahan *ed* Seth Holt *m* William Alwyn. *LP*: Mandy Miller, Phyllis Calvert, Jack Hawkins, Terence Morgan, Godfrey Tearle.

Meet Me in St Louis (USA 1944: 118 mins).
MGM *dir* Vincente Minnelli *prod* Arthur Freed *scr* Irvin Brechner, Fred F. Finklehoffe, from the book by Sally Benson *phot* George Folsey *art dir* Cedric Gibbons, Lemuel Ayers, Jack Martin Smith *ed* Albert Akst *m* Georgie Stoll. *LP*: Judy Garland, Margaret O'Brien, Mary Astor, Leon Armes, Lucille Bremner, Marjorie Main, Harry Davenport, Tom Drake, Hugh Marlowe.

The Member of the Wedding (USA 1953: 91 mins).
Columbia *dir* Fred Zinnemann *prod* Stanley Kramer *scr* Edna and Edward Anhalt, from the novel and play by Carson McCullers *phot* Hal Mohr *art dir* Rudolph Sternad *ed* William Lyon *m* Alex North. *LP*: Julie Harris, Ethel Waters, Brandon de Wilde.

The Miracle Worker (USA 1962: 106 mins).
United Artists *dir* Arthur Penn *prod* Fred Coe *scr* William Gibson, based on his play *phot* Ernest Capaross *art dir* George Jenkins, Mel Bourne *ed* Aram Avakiam *m* Laurence Rosenthal. *LP*: Anne Bancroft, Patty Duke, Victor Jory, Inga Swenson, Andrew Prine.

Mirror (USSR 1975: 106 mins).
Mosfilm *dir* Andrei Tarkovsky *scr* Andrei Tarkovsky, Alexandr Misharin *phot* Georgi Rerberg *art dir* Nikolai Dvigubsky *ed* L. Feiginova *m* Eduard Artemiev, J. S. Bach, Pergolesi, Purcell. *LP*: Margarita Terekhova, Filip Yankovsky, Ignat Daniltsev, Oleg Yankovsky.

Les Mistons: The Mischief Makers (France 1958: 26 mins).
Les Films du Carosse *dir, scr* François Truffaut, from the short story 'Virginales'

by Maurice Pons *phot* Jean Maligo *ed* Cecile Decugis *m* Maurice Le Roux. *LP*: Bernadette Lafont, Gerard Blain.

The Nanny (GB 1965: 93 mins).
Hammer Films *dir* Seth Holt *prod, scr* Jimmy Sangster, from the novel by Evelyn Piper *phot* Harry Waxman *art dir* Edward Carrick *ed* Tom Simpson, James Needs *m* Richard Rodney Bennett. *LP*: Bette Davis, Wendy Craig, James Villiers, William Dix, Jill Bennett, Pamela Franklin, Maurice Denham.

The Night of the Hunter (USA 1955: 91 mins).
United Artists *dir* Charles Laughton *prod* Paul Gregory *scr* James Agee, Davis Grubb, from the novel by Davis Grubb *phot* Stanley Cortez *art dir* Hilyard Brown *ed* Robert Golden *m* Walter Schumann. *LP*: Robert Mitchum, Lillian Gish, Shelley Winters, Billy Chapin, Peter Graves, James Gleason, Evelyn Varden.

Los Olvidados: The Young and the Damned (Mexico 1950: 88 mins).
Ultramar Films *dir* Luis Buñuel *prod* Oscar Dancigers *scr* Luis Buñuel, Luis Alcoriza *phot* Gabriel Figueroa *art dir* Edward Fitzgerald *ed* Carlos Savage *m* Rodolfo Halftter. *LP*: Alfonso Mejia, Roberto Cobo, Estela Inda, Miguel Inclán.

Radio Days (USA 1987: 85 mins).
Orion *dir, scr* Woody Allen *prod* Roger Greenhut *phot* Carlo di Palma *art dir* Santo Loquasto *ed* Susan Morse *m* Dick Hyman. *LP*: Mia Farrow, Seth Green, Julie Kavner, Michael Tucker, Dianne Wiest, Josh Mostel, Wallace Shawn, Diane Keaton.

The Red Balloon (France 1956: 35 mins).
Films Montsouris *dir, scr* Albert Lamorisse *phot* Edmond Sechan *ed* Pierre Gillette *m* Maurice Le Roux. *LP*: Pascal Lamorisse.

River's Edge (USA 1986: 99 mins).
Hemdale *dir* Tim Hunter *prod* Sarah Pillsbury, Midge Sanford *scr* Neal Jimenez *phot* Frederick Elmes *art dir* John Moto *ed*

Howard Smith, Sonya Sones *m* Jurgen Knieper. *LP*: Crispin Glover, Keanu Reeves, Ione Skye, David Roebuck, Joshua Miller, Dennis Hopper.

The Search (USA/Switzerland 1948: 105 mins).
MGN *dir* Fred Zinnemann *prod* Latar Wechsler *scr* Richard Schweizer, David Wechsler *phot* Emil Berna *ed* Hermann Haller *m* Robert Blum. *LP*: Montgomery Clift, Wendell Corey, Aline McMahon, Jarmila Novotna, Ivan Jandl.

Shane (USA 1953: 118 mins).
Paramount *dir, prod* George Stevens *scr* A. B. Guthrie Jr, from the novel by Jack Schaefer *phot* Loyal Griggs *art dir* Hal Pereira, Walter Tyler *ed* William Hornbeck, Tom McAdoo *m* Victor Young. *LP*: Alan Ladd, Van Heflin, Jean Arthur, Brandon de Wilde, Jack Palance, Emile Meyer, Ben Johnson, Elisha Cook Jr.

Stand by Me (USA 1986: 88 mins).
Columbia *dir* Rob Reiner *prod* Bruce A. Evans, Raynold Gideon, Andrew Scheinman *scr* Raynold Gideon, Bruce A. Evans, from the novella *The Body* by Stephen King *phot* Thomas del Ruth *art dir* Dennis Washington *ed* Robert Leighton *m* Jack Nitzsche. *LP*: Will Wheaton, River Phoenix, Corey Feldman, Jerry O'Connell, Richard Dreyfuss, Kiefer Sutherland.

Toto the Hero (Belgium 1991: 91 mins).
Iblis Films *dir, scr* Jaco Van Dormael *prod* Pierre Drouot, Dany Geys *phot* Walther van den Ende *art dir* Hubert Pouille *ed* Susana Rossberg *m* Pierre Van Dormael. *LP*: Michel Bouquet, Thomas Godet, Mireille Perrier, Klaus Schindler, Fabienne Loriaux, Sandrine Blancke.

A World Apart (GB 1988: 113 mins).
British Screen/Working Title/Film Four *dir* Chris Menges *prod* Sarah Radclyffe *scr* Shawn Slovo *phot* Peter Biziou *art dir* Brian Morris *ed* Nicholas Gaster *m* Hans Zimmer. *LP*: Barbara Hershey, Jodhi May, David Suchet, Jeroen Krabbe, Paul Freeman.

NOTES

CHAPTER ONE
1   Jack Schaefer, *Shane*, Corgi, 1951, p. 134
2   François Truffaut, *The Films in my Life*, Penguin, 1982, p. 222
3   David Shipman, *The Story of Cinema*, Vol. 2, Hodder & Stoughton, 1984, p. 1211
4   *Sight and Sound*, Summer 1985, p. 180

CHAPTER TWO
1   Sylvia Plath, *The Bell-Jar*, Faber, 1963, p. 34
2   *Agee on Film*, Peter Owen, 1963, p. 302
3   *Film: Book 1*, Ed. Robert Hughes, Grove Press, 1959, p.41
4   Pauline Kael, *I Lost it at the Movies*, Bantam, 1966, p. 100
5   Andrei Tarkovsky, *Sculpting in Time*, Bodley Head, 1986, p. 17
6   *Magills Survey of Cinema*, Salem Press, 1988, p. 170
7   *Hope and Glory*, Screenplay, Faber, 1987, p. 23
8   John Boorman, Introduction to *Hope and Glory*, Faber, p. 8
9   John Boorman, *Hope and Glory*, p. 9
10 *The Independent*, 23 March 1988, p. 13
11 *The Guardian*, 17 March 1988, p. 11

CHAPTER THREE
1   *Anatomy of the Movies*, Ed. David Pirie, Windward, 1980, p. 262
2   Graham Greene, *The Pleasure Dome*, Secker & Warburg, 1972, p. 72
3   Michel Ciment, *John Boorman*, Faber, 1986, p. 164
4   R. S. Prawer, *Caligari's Children*, Oxford, 1986, p. 71

CHAPTER FOUR
1   *A Critical History of the British Cinema*, Secker & Warburg, 1978, p. 266
2   *Sight and Sound*, Winter 1988/9, p. 52
3   François Truffaut, *The Films in my Life*, Penguin, 1982, p. 199
4   Louis Giannetti, *Masters of the American Cinema*, Prentice Hall, 1981, p. 379

CHAPTER FIVE
1   D. H. Lawrence, *Sons and Lovers*, Penguin, 1967, p. 62
2   *Agee on Film*, Peter Owen, 1963, p. 356
3   Vincente Minnelli, *I Remember it Well*, Angus & Robertson, 1975, p. 129
4   *Genre: The Musical*, Ed. Rick Attman, Routledge & Kegan Paul, 1981, p. 20

CHAPTER SIX
1   David Thomson, *America in the Dark*, Hutchinson, 1978, p. 169
2   Graham Greene, *The Pleasure Dome*, Secker & Warburg, 1972, p. 180
3   James Baldwin, *The Devil Finds Work*, Michael Joseph, 1976, p. 26
4   T. E. B. Clarke, *This is where I came in*, Michael Joseph, 1974, p. 155

5   *The Exterminating Angel/Nazarin/Los Olvidados: Three Films by Luis Buñuel*, Lorrimer Modern Film Scripts, 1972, p. 217
6   *Three Films by Luis Buñuel*, Lorrimer, 1972, p. 238
7   James Monaco, *American Film Now*, Plume, 1979, p. 365
8   R. P. Kolker, *A Cinema of Loneliness*, Oxford, 1980, pp. 258–9
9   Arthur Miller, *Timebends*, Methuen, 1987, p. 501
10 *Monthly Film Bulletin*, October 1987, p. 296

CHAPTER SEVEN
1   André Bazin, *Orson Welles*, Elm Tree Books, 1978, p. 66
2   Graham Greene, *A Sort of Life*, Bodley Head, 1971, p. 39
3   Graham Greene, *Collected Short Stories*, Penguin, 1985, p. 110
4   Richard Hughes, *A High Wind in Jamaica*, Chatto & Windus, 1975, pp. 182–3
5   *Sight and Sound*, Winter 1973/4, p. 7

CHAPTER EIGHT
1   *Sight and Sound*, Spring 1976, p. 95
2   Andrei Tarkovsky, *Sculpting in Time*, Bodley Head, 1986, p. 130
3   Andrei Tarkovsky, *Sculpting in Time*, p. 128
4   *Cinema Papers*, July 1986, p. 23

SELECT BIBLIOGRAPHY

James Baldwin, *The Devil Finds Work*, Michael Joseph, 1976.
John Boorman, *Hope and Glory: Screenplay*, Faber, 1987.
Peter Coveney, *The Image of Childhood*, Peregrine Books, 1967.
Lionel Godfrey, 'Because They're Young,' *Films & Filming*, Oct & Nov, 1967.
Graham Greene, *A Sort of Life*, Bodley Head, 1971.
R. P. Kolker, *The Altering Eye*, Oxford University Press, 1983.
David Lusted (ed.) *Kidstuff: Childhood and Cinema*, BFI, 1979.
James Monaco, *American Film Now*, Oxford University Press, 1979.
S. S. Prawer, *Caligari's Children*, Oxford University Press, 1980.
Jacqueline Rose, *The Case of Peter Pan*, Macmillan, 1984.
Andrei Tarkovsky, *Sculpting in Time*, Bodley Head, 1986.
François Truffaut, *The Films in my Life*, Penguin, 1982.
Robin Wood, *Personal Views*, Gordon Fraser, 1976.

INDEX

INDEX